Contents

Introduction

"God is love": those three words could hardly be more bouncy. They seem lively, lovely and as warming as a crackling fire. But "God is a Trinity"? No, hardly the same effect: that just sounds cold and stodgy. All quite understandable, but the aim of this book is to stop the madness. Yes, the Trinity can be presented as a fusty and irrelevant dogma, but the truth is that God is love *because* God is a Trinity.

This book, then, will simply be about growing in our enjoyment of God and seeing how God's triune being makes all his ways beautiful. It is a chance to taste and see that the Lord is good, to have your heart won and yourself refreshed. For it is only when you grasp what it means for God to be a Trinity that you really sense the beauty, the overflowing kindness, the heart-grabbing loveliness of God. If the Trinity were something we could shave off God, we would not be relieving him of some irksome weight; we would be shearing him of precisely what is so delightful about him. For God *is* triune, and it is *as triune* that he is so good and desirable.

But I must congratulate you for having read so far as this. The Christian books that really fly off the shelves are the "how to" books, the ones that give you something immediate to *do*. And to the "how to" junkies, the thought of reading a book on the Trinity must feel like having to say "Theodore Oswaldtwistle the thistle sifter sifted a sack of thistles"—rather hard going but pointless. Yet Christianity is not primarily about lifestyle change; it is about knowing God. To know and grow to enjoy him is what we are saved *for*—and that is what we are going to press into here.

Nonetheless, getting to know God better does actually make for far more profound and practical change *as well*. Knowing the love of God is the very thing that makes us loving. Sensing the desirability of God alters our preferences and inclinations, the things that drive our behavior: we begin to *want* God more than anything else. Thus, to read this book is not to play an intellectual game. In fact, we will see that the triune nature of this God affects everything from how we listen to music to how we pray: it makes for happier marriages, warmer dealings with others, better church life; it gives Christians assurance, shapes holiness and transforms the very way we look at the world around us. No exaggeration: the knowledge of this God turns lives around.

Spooky, Huh?

There is, of course, that major obstacle in our way: that the Trinity is seen not as a solution and a delight, but as an oddity and a problem. In fact, some of the ways people talk about the Trinity only seem to reinforce the idea. Think, for example, of all those desperate-sounding illustrations. "The Trinity," some helpful soul explains, "is a bit like an egg, where there is the shell, the yolk and the white, and yet it is all one egg!" "No," says another, "the Trinity is more like a shamrock leaf: that's one leaf, but it's got three bits sticking out. *Just* like the Father, Son and Spirit." And one wonders why the world laughs. For whether the Trinity is compared to shrubbery, streaky bacon, the three states of H_2O or a three-headed giant, it begins to sound, well, bizarre, like some pointless and unsightly growth on our understanding of God, one that could surely be lopped off with no consequence other than a universal sigh of relief.

DELIGHTING
IN THE TRINITY

An Introduction to the Christian Faith

MICHAEL REEVES

IVP Academic

An imprint of InterVarsity Press
Downers Grove, Illinois

InterVarsity Press
P.O. Box 1400, Downers Grove, IL 60515-1426
ivpress.com
email@ivpress.com

©2012 by Michael Reeves

Published in the United States of America by InterVarsity Press, Downers Grove, Illinois, with permisssion from Paternoster Press.

Published in the United Kingdom as The Good God.

InterVarsity Press® is the book-publishing division of InterVarsity Christian Fellowship/USA®, a movement of students and faculty active on campus at hundreds of universities, colleges and schools of nursing in the United States of America, and a member movement of the International Fellowship of Evangelical Students. For information about local and regional activities, visit www.intervarsity.org.

All Scripture quotations, unless otherwise indicated, are taken from the Holy Bible, New International Version®. NIV®. Copyright ©1973, 1978, 1984 by International Bible Society. Used by permission of Zondervan Publishing House. All rights reserved.

Cover design: Cindy Kiple
Images: Marion Boddy-Evans/Getty Images
Interior design: Beth McGill

ISBN 978-0-8308-3983-4 (print)
ISBN 978-0-8308-6673-1 (digital)

Printed in the United States of America ∞

InterVarsity Press is committed to ecological stewardship and to the conservation of natural resources in all our operations. This book was printed using sustainably sourced paper.

Library of Congress Cataloging-in-Publication Data

Reeves, Michael, Dr.
  Delighting in the Trinity : an introduction to the Christian faith /
Michael Reeves.
    p. cm.
  Includes bibliographical references and index.
  ISBN 978-0-8308-3983-4 (pbk. : alk. paper)
  1. Trinity. 2. Theology, Doctrinal. I. Title.

  BT111.3.R44 2012
  230—dc23

                                                    2012018665

P   34   33   32   31   30

Y   34   33   32   31   30   29   28   27   26   25   24   23   22

My dear Mia,

*My great love for you is but a spark from
the mighty flame of love you can read about here.
I hope this will help you enjoy a Father's love.*

Now, of course, if the Trinity is seen as a weird and fantastic monstrosity, then small wonder it is seen as irrelevant. How could the eggishness of God ever be more than a weird curiosity? I am never going to fall down in awe or find my heart drawn to a God so ridiculous. And yet in many ways that is just where we are today. For all that we may give an orthodox nod of the head to belief in the Trinity, it simply seems too arcane to make any practical difference to our lives. In other words, the egg illustration and its kind may not be the way to go.

Another way to go that can reinforce the idea that the Trinity is essentially a problem is to stick solely to saying what the Trinity is not. We explain that the Father is not the Son, the Spirit is not the Father, there are not three gods and so on. All of which is true, but it can leave one with the hollow sense that one has successfully avoided all sorts of nasty-sounding heresies, but at the cost of wondering who or what one is actually to worship.

Enter the word *mystery,* a word so soothing it lets us feel that our absolute cluelessness about how God can be both one and three is actually how things are supposed to be. "God is a mystery," we can whisper in our most piously hushed tones. "We are simply not meant to know such things." But while such sentiments score high for their ring of reverence, they score pretty low for accuracy. When in Ephesians 3, for example, Paul writes of the "mystery" that the Gentiles are now included in salvation, the word *mystery* simply  means secret. Paul is sharing a secret with us. Now we know. We are not left wondering what he could possibly mean. The Gentiles are now included. There is nothing we would call "mysterious" about this mystery.

So it is with God. God *is* a mystery, but not in the alien abductions, things-that-go-bump-in-the-night sense. Certainly not in the "who can know, why bother?" sense. God is a mystery in that who he is and what he is like are secrets, things we would never have worked out by ourselves. But this triune God has revealed himself to us. Thus the Trinity is not some piece of inexplicable apparent nonsense, like a square circle or an interesting theologian. Rather, because the triune God has revealed himself, we can understand the Trinity. That is not to say we can exhaust our knowledge of God, comprehend and wrap our brains around him, simply cramming in a few bits of information before moving on to some other doctrine. To know the Trinity is to know God, an eternal and personal God of infinite beauty, interest and fascination. The Trinity is a God we *can* know, and forever grow to know better.

All of which is to say, the Trinity is not a problem. In looking at the Trinity we are not walking off the map into dangerous and unchartable areas of pointless speculation. Far, far from it. Pressing into the Trinity we are doing what in Psalm 27 David said he could do all the days of his life: we are gazing upon the beauty of the Lord. And as we do so, I hope you will begin to feel as David did, and that you could do the same.

Bored Monks on Rainy Afternoons

There is one other problem people can have with the Trinity: that the word never appears in the Bible. Now that doesn't sound good, and it's given rise to the legend of the Trinity as the invention of some cloister-bound theologians with too much time on their hands. The story goes that the Bible knows only a simple, boiled-down monotheism, but that with some ingenuity, wild speculation and a whole lot of philosophical rigamarole, the church managed to cook up this knotty and perplexing dish, the Trinity.

That just isn't how the history goes, though. The apostle Paul, for example, didn't show any sign of struggle to confess "that Jesus Christ is Lord, to the glory of God the Father" (Phil 2:11). You don't see a cloudy ignorance of the Father, Son and Spirit in A.D. 50 which is all cleared up by A.D. 500. And while later church theologians would use philosophical terms and words not seen in the Bible (like *Trinity*), they were not trying to *add* to God's revelation of himself, as if Scripture were insufficient; they were trying to express the truth of who God is *as revealed in Scripture*. Particularly, they were trying to articulate Scripture's message in the face of those who were distorting it in one way or another—and for each new distortion a new language of response was needed.

Quite deliberately, then, I want to demonstrate that, through and through, the Trinity is a *scriptural* truth—and I want even the layout of the book to make that clear. So we'll get to hear from many of the great minds who've thought on this, but I want to

---

SCRIPTURAL, REALLY?

"Then what about Deuteronomy 6:4?" I hear my many Muslim readers cry. "Hear, O Israel: The LORD our God, the LORD is *one*." One, not three. But the point of Deuteronomy 6:4 is not to teach that "The LORD our God, the LORD is a mathematical singularity." In the middle of Deuteronomy 6, that would be a bit out of the blue to say the least. Instead, Deuteronomy 6 is about God's people having the Lord as the *one* object of their affections: he is the only one worthy of them, and they are to love him alone with all their heart, soul and strength (Deut 6:5). In fact, the word for "one" in Deuteronomy 6:4 really doesn't convey "mathematical singularity" at all well. The word is also used, for example, in Genesis 2:24, where Adam and Eve—*two* persons—are said to be *one*.

We'll be looking at many such verses, and through them all I think it will become clear: the more we push into the Scriptures, the more we see that the God they present really is triune.

avoid giving the impression that they were at some higher stage of religious evolution than the Bible. They were mere heralds of the triune God revealed in Scripture.

The Christian Distinctive

Exactly how important is the Trinity, though? Is it the sticky toffee pudding of faith—a nice way to round things off, but incidental—or is it the main course? Steel yourself for the thunders of the Athanasian Creed, a statement of faith from the fifth or sixth century, which begins: "Whosoever will be saved, before all things it is necessary that he hold the catholic [that is, the church's orthodox] faith; which faith except every one do keep whole and undefiled, without doubt he shall perish everlastingly. And the catholic faith is this: that we worship one God in Trinity, and Trinity in Unity."

Now today that sounds overwrought to the point of being hysterical. We must believe in the Trinity or "perish everlastingly"? No, that goes too far, surely? For while we might be happy enough to include the Trinity in our list of "things Christians believe," the suggestion that our very salvation depends on the Trinity comes across as ridiculously overinflated bluster. How could something so curious be necessary for salvation "before all things"?

And yet. The unflinching boldness of the Athanasian Creed forces us to ask what is essential for Christian faith. What would *we* say is the article of faith that must be held before all others? Salvation by grace alone? Christ's atoning work on the cross? His bodily resurrection? Now certainly those are all things "of first importance" (1 Cor 15:3), so absolutely critical that they cannot be given up without the very nature and goodness of the gospel being lost; however, they do not stand "before all things." By themselves they are not what make the Christian gospel Christian. Jehovah's Witnesses can believe in the sacrificial death of Christ; Mormons in his resurrection; others in salvation by grace. Granted, the sim-

THE PROTESTANT BUDDHISTS

Francis Xavier was a Roman Catholic missionary to Asia. When he reached Japan in 1549 he came across a particular sect of Buddhism *(Yodo Shin-Shu)* that stank, he said, of what he called "the Lutheran heresy." That is, like the Reformer Martin Luther, these Buddhists believed in salvation by grace alone and not by human effort. Simple trust in Amida, they held, instead of trust in self, was sufficient to achieve rebirth into the pure land. If we call on him, they taught, then despite our failings, all his achievements become ours.

Of course, the "salvation" in view here was nothing like Christian salvation: it was not about knowing Amida or being known by him; it was about enlightenment and the achievement of Nirvana. It was, nonetheless, a salvation grounded on the virtues and achievements of another, and appropriated by faith alone.

ilarities are sometimes only superficial, but the very fact that certain Christian beliefs can be shared by other belief systems shows that they cannot be the foundation on which the Christian gospel rests, the truth that stands "before all things."

We need not be disturbed by such similarities. That which distinguishes Christianity has not been stolen. For what makes Christianity absolutely distinct is the identity of our God. *Which* God we worship: *that* is the article of faith that stands before all others. The bedrock of our faith is nothing less than God himself, and every aspect of the

Francis Xavier (1506-1552)

gospel—creation, revelation, salvation—is only Christian insofar as it is the creation, revelation and salvation of *this* God, the triune God. I could believe in the death of a man called Jesus, I could believe in his bodily resurrection, I could even believe in a salvation by grace alone; but if I do not believe in this God, then, quite simply, I am not a Christian. And so, because the Christian God is triune, the Trinity is the governing center of all Christian belief, the truth that shapes and beautifies all others. The Trinity is the cockpit of all Christian thinking.

Can't We Get Along with Just "God"?

Strangely enough, who and what God is like tend to be things we assume we already know and so do not need to think much more about. Especially in the post-Christian West, where the identity of God seems to have been pretty much universally agreed on for centuries, it seems obvious. Thus Christians ask non-Christians whether they believe in "God"—as if the very idea of "God" is self-explanatory, as if we will all be thinking of the same sort of being.

Yet the temptation to sculpt God according to our expectations and presuppositions, to make this God much like another, is strong with us. You see it all down through history: in the Middle Ages it seemed obvious for people to think of God as a feudal lord; the first missionaries to the Vikings thought it obvious to present Christ as a warrior God, an axe-wielding divine berserker who could out-Odin Odin. And so on. The trouble is, the triune God simply does not fit well into the mold of any other God. Trying to get along with some unspecified "God," we will quickly find ourselves with *another* God.

That, ironically, is often why we struggle with the Trinity: instead of starting from scratch and seeing that the triune God is a radically different sort of being from any other candidate for "God," we try to stuff Father, Son and Spirit into how we have always thought of God. Now, usually in the West, "God" is already a subtly defined idea: it refers to one person, not three. So when we come to the Trinity, we feel like we're trying to squeeze two extra persons into our understanding of God—and that is, to say the least, rather hard. And hard things get left. The Trinity becomes that awkward appendix.

So used are we to fashioning God according to our assumptions that our minds simply rebel at the thought of a God who is not as we would expect. We imagine God would be a simpler being—a single-person God. Perhaps, then, it is not so much the seemingly bad math of the Trinity that puts us off as the sheer imposition of an unexpected sort of God.

And it is not just that we are quick to replace the living God with gods of our devising: the world is already filled with innumerable, often wildly different candidates for "God." Some are good, some are not. Some are personal, some are not. Some are omnipotent, some are not. You see it in the Bible, where the Lord God of Israel, Baal, Dagon, Molech and Artemis are completely different. Or take, for example, how the Qur'an explicitly and sharply distinguishes Allah from the God described by Jesus:

> Say not "Trinity." Desist; it will be better for you: for God is one God. Glory be to Him: (far exalted is He) above having a son.[1]

> Say: "He, Allah, is One.
> Allah is He on Whom all depend.
> *He begets not, nor is He begotten.*
> And none is like Him."[2]

In other words, Allah is a single-person God. In no sense is he a Father ("he begets not"), and in no sense does he have a Son ("nor is he begotten"). He is one person, and not three. Allah, then,

---

[1]Surah 4.171.
[2]Surah 112, my emphasis.

is an utterly different sort of being to the God who is Father, Son
and Spirit. And it is not just incompatibly different numbers we
are dealing with here: that difference, as we will see, is going to
mean that Allah exists and functions in a completely different way
from the Father, Son and Spirit.

All that being the case, it would be madness to settle for any
presupposed idea of God. Without being specific about which
God is God, which God will we worship? Which God will we ever
call others to worship? Given all the different preconceptions
people have about "God," it simply will not do for us to speak ab-
stractly about some general "God." And where would doing so
leave us? If we content ourselves with being mere monotheists,
and speak of God only in terms so vague they could apply to Allah
as much as the Trinity, then we will never enjoy or share what is
so fundamentally and delightfully different about Christianity.

The Shocking Joy

The irony could not be thicker: what we assume would be a dull or
peculiar irrelevance turns out to be the source of all that is good
in Christianity. Neither a problem nor a technicality, the triune
being of God is the vital oxygen of Christian life and joy. And so it
is my hope and prayer that as you read this book, the knowledge
of Father, Son and Spirit will breathe fresh life into you.

What Was God Doing Before Creation?

The Dark Path and the Bright Lane

There are two very different ways or approaches to thinking about God. The first way is like a slippery, sloping cliff-top goat path. On a stormy, moonless night. During an earthquake. It is the path of trying to work God out by our own brainpower. I look around at the world and sense it must have all come from somewhere. Someone or something caused it to be, and that someone I will call God. God, then, is the one who brings everything else into existence, but who is not himself brought into being by anything. He is the uncaused cause. That is *who he is*. God *is,* essentially, The Creator, The One in Charge.

It all sounds very reasonable and unobjectionable, but if I do start there, with that as my basic view of God, I will find every inch of my Christianity covered and wasted by the nastiest toxic fallout. First of all, if God's very identity is to be The Creator, The Ruler, then he needs a creation to rule *in order to be who he is.* For all his cosmic power, then, this God turns out to be pitifully weak: he *needs* us. And yet you'd struggle to find the pity in you, given what he's like. In the aftermath of World War II, the twentieth-century Swiss theologian Karl Barth put it starkly:

> Perhaps you recall how, when Hitler used to speak about God, he called Him "the Almighty". But it is not "the Almighty" who is God; we cannot understand from the standpoint of a

supreme concept of power, who God is. And the man who calls "the Almighty" God misses God in the most terrible way. For "the Almighty" is bad, as "power in itself" is bad. The "Almighty" means Chaos, Evil, the Devil. We could not better describe and define the Devil than by trying to think this idea of a self-based, free, sovereign ability.[1]

Now Barth was absolutely not denying that God is Almighty; but he wanted to make very clear that mere might is not who God is.

The problems don't stop there, though: if God's very identity is to be The Ruler, what kind of salvation can he offer me (if he's even prepared to offer such a thing)? If God is The Ruler and the problem is that I have broken the rules, the only salvation he can offer is to forgive me and treat me as if I had kept the rules.

But if that is how God is, my relationship with him can be little better than my relationship with any traffic cop (meaning no offense to any readers in the police force). Let me put it like this: if, as never happens, some fine cop were to catch me speeding and so breaking the rules, I would be punished; if, as never happens, he failed to spot me or I managed to shake him off after an exciting car chase, I would be relieved. But in neither case would I love him. And even if, like God, he chose to let me off the hook for my law-breaking, I still would not love him. I might feel grateful, and that gratitude might be deep, but that is not at all the same thing as love. And so it is with the divine policeman: if salvation simply means him letting me off and counting me as a law-abiding citizen, then gratitude (not love) is all I have. In other words, I can never really love the God who is essentially just The Ruler. And that, ironically, means I can never keep the greatest command: to love the Lord my God. Such is the cold and gloomy place to which the dark goat path takes us.

The other way to think about God is lamp-lit and evenly paved: it is Jesus Christ, the Son of God. It is, in fact, The Way. It is a lane

---

[1]Karl Barth, *Dogmatics in Outline*, trans. G. T. Thompson (London: SCM Press, 1949), p. 48.

that ends happily in a very different place, with a very different sort of God. How? Well, just the fact that Jesus is "the Son" really says it all. Being a Son means he has a Father. The God he reveals is, first and foremost, a Father. "I am the way and the truth and the life," he says. "No one comes to the Father except through me" (Jn 14:6). That is who God has revealed himself to be: not first and foremost Creator or Ruler, but Father.

Perhaps the way to appreciate this best is to ask what God was doing before creation. Now to the followers of the goat path that is an absurd, impossible question to answer; their wittiest theologians reply with the put-down: "What was God doing before creation? Making hell for those cheeky enough to ask such questions!" But on the lane it is an easy question to answer. Jesus tells us explicitly in John 17:24. "Father," he says, "you loved me before the creation of the world." And that is the God revealed by Jesus Christ. Before he ever created, before he ever ruled the world, before anything else, this God was a Father loving his Son.

"HE STOOD FOR THE TRINITARIAN DOCTRINE"

At the beginning of the fourth century, in Alexandria in the north of Egypt, a theologian named Arius began teaching that the Son was a created being, and not truly God. He did so because he believed that God is the origin and cause of everything, but is not caused to exist by anything else. "Uncaused" or "Unoriginate," he therefore held, was the best basic definition of what God is like. But since the Son, being a son, must have *received* his being from the Father, he could not, by Arius's definition, be God.

The argument persuaded many; it did not persuade Arius's brilliant young contemporary, Athanasius. Believing that Arius had started in the wrong place with his basic definition of God, Athanasius dedicated the rest of his life to proving how catastrophic Arius's thinking was for healthy Christian living.

Actually, I've put it much too mildly: Athanasius simply boggled at

Icon of St. Athanasius
(296?-373)

Arius's presumption. How could he possibly know what God is like other than as he has revealed himself? "It is," he said, "more pious and more accurate to signify God from the Son and call Him Father, than to name Him from His works only and call Him Unoriginate."[a] That is to say, the right way to think about God is to start with Jesus Christ, the Son of God, not some abstract definition we have made up like "Uncaused" or "Unoriginate." In fact, we should not even set out in our understanding of God by thinking of God primarily as Creator (naming him "from His works only")—that, as we have seen, would make him dependent on his creation. Our definition of God must be built on the Son who reveals him. And when we do that, starting with the Son, we find that the first thing to say about God is, as it says in the creed, "We believe in one God, *the Father.*"

That different starting point and basic understanding of God would mean that the gospel Athanasius preached simply felt and tasted very different from the one preached by Arius. Arius would have to pray to "Unoriginate." But would "Unoriginate" listen? Athanasius could pray "Our Father." With "The Unoriginate" we are left scrambling for a dictionary in a philosophy lecture; with a Father things are familial. And if God is a Father, then he must be relational and life-giving, and *that* is the sort of God we could love.

---

[a]Athanasius, *Against the Arians* 1.34.

The Loving Father

The most foundational thing in God is not some abstract quality, but the fact that he is Father. Again and again, the Scriptures equate the terms *God* and *Father:* in Exodus, the Lord calls Israel "my firstborn son" (Ex 4:22; see also Is 1:2; Jer 31:9; Hos 11:1); he carries his people "as a father carries his son" (Deut 1:31), disciplines them "as a man disciplines his son" (Deut 8:5); he calls to them, saying: "As a father has compassion on his children, so the LORD has compassion on those who fear him" (Ps 103:13) and "'How gladly would I treat you like sons and give you a desirable land, the most beautiful inheritance of any nation.' I thought you would call me 'Father' and not turn away from following me" (Jer 3:19; see also Jer 3:4; Deut 32:6; Mal 1:6).

Isaiah thus prays, "You are our Father, . . . you, O LORD, are our Father" (Is 63:16; see also Is 64:8); and a popular Old Testament name was Abijah ("The Lord is my father"). Then Jesus repeatedly refers to God as "the Father" and directs prayer to "our Father"; he tells his disciples he will return to "my Father and your Father, to my God and your God" (Jn 20:17); Paul and Peter refer to "the God and Father of our Lord Jesus Christ" (Rom 15:6; 1 Pet 1:3); Paul writes of "one God, the Father" (1 Cor 8:6), of "God our Father and the Lord Jesus Christ" (1 Cor 1:3); Hebrews counsels: "God is treating you as sons. For what son is not disciplined by his father?" (Heb 12:7).

Since God is, before all things, a Father, and not primarily Creator or Ruler, all his ways are beautifully fatherly. It is not that this God "does" being Father as a day job, only to kick back in the evenings as plain old "God." It is not that he has a nice blob of fatherly icing on top. He *is* Father. All the way down. Thus all that he does he does as Father. That is who he is. He creates as a Father and he rules as a Father; and that means the way he rules over creation is most unlike the way any other God would rule over creation. The French Reformer John Calvin, appreciating this deeply, once wrote:

> We ought in the very order of things [in creation] diligently to contemplate God's fatherly love . . . [for as] a foreseeing and diligent father of the family he shows his wonderful goodness toward us. . . . To conclude once for all, whenever we call God the Creator of heaven and earth, let us at the same time bear in mind that . . . we are indeed his children, whom he has received into his faithful protection to nourish and educate. . . . So, invited by the great sweetness of his beneficence and goodness, let us study to love and serve him with all our heart.[2]

It was a profound observation, for it is only when we see that God rules his creation *as a kind and loving Father* that we will be moved to delight in his providence. We might acknowledge that the rule of some heavenly policeman was just, but we could never take delight in his regime as we can delight in the tender care of a father.

So what *does* it mean that God is a Father? Well, first of all, it does actually mean something. Not all names do. My dog is called Max, but that doesn't really tell you anything about him. The name doesn't tell you what he is or what he's like. But—if I can make the jump—the Father is called Father because he *is* a Father. And a father is a person who gives life, who begets children. Now that insight is like a stick of dynamite in all our thoughts about God. For if, before all things, God was eternally a Father, then this God is an inherently outgoing, life-giving God. He did not give life for the first time when he decided to create; from eternity he has been life-giving.

This gets unpacked for us in 1 John 4: "Dear friends, let us love one another, for love comes from God. Everyone who loves has been born of God and knows God. Whoever does not love does not know God, because God is love" (1 Jn 4:7-8).

---

[2]John Calvin, *Institutes of the Christian Religion* 1.14.2, 22.

WHEN "FATHER" IS A BAD THING

Not everyone instinctively warms to the idea that God is a Father. There are many for whom their own experiences of overbearing, indifferent or abusive fathers make their very guts squirm when they hear God spoken of as a Father. The twentieth-century French philosopher Michel Foucault had very much that sort of issue. The bulk of his life's work was about the evils of authority, and it seems to have all started with the first figure of authority in his life: his father. Fearful of having some namby-pamby for a son, Foucault Senior—who was a surgeon—did what he could to "toughen up" the little mite. That meant, for example, ghoulishly forcing him to witness an amputation. "The image, certainly, has all the ingredients of a recurrent nightmare: the sadistic father, the impotent child, the knife slicing into flesh, the body cut to the bone, the demand to acknowledge the sovereign power of the patriarch, and the inexpressible humiliation of the son, having his manliness put to the test."[a]

For Foucault, paternal power had not been used to care, to nurture and to bless, and so for him the word *father* came to be associated with a host of dark images.

One's heart goes out to the children of such fathers, and those of us who are fathers ourselves know that we too are far from perfect. But God the Father is not called Father because he copies earthly fathers. He is not some pumped-up version of your dad. To transfer the failings of earthly fathers to him is, quite simply, a misstep. Instead, things are the other way around: it is that all human fathers are *supposed* to reflect him—only where some do that well, others do a better job of reflecting the devil.

---

[a]James Miller, *The Passion of Michel Foucault* (New York: Simon & Schuster, 1993), p. 366.

Have you ever known someone so magnetically kind and gracious, so warm and generous of spirit that just a little time spent with them affects how you think, feel and behave? Someone whose very presence makes you better—even if only for a while, when you are with them? I know people like that, and they seem to be little pictures of how God is, according to John. This God, he says, is love in such a profound and potent way that you simply cannot know him without yourself becoming loving.

This is precisely what it means for God to be Father. For when John writes "God is love" at the end of verse 8, he is clearly referring to the Father. His very next words, in verse 9, state: "This is how God showed his love among us: *He sent his one and only Son*." The God who is love is the Father who sends his Son. To be the Father, then, *means* to love, to give out life, to beget the Son. Before anything else, for all eternity, this God was loving, giving life to and delighting in his Son.

Seeing this, many theologians have liked to compare the Father to a fountain, ever bursting out with life and love (indeed, the Lord calls himself "the spring of living water" in Jeremiah 2:13, and the image crops up again and again in Scripture). And just as a fountain, to be a fountain, must pour forth water, so the Father, to be Father, must give out life. That is who he is. That is his most fundamental identity. Thus love is not something the Father *has*, merely one of his many moods. Rather, he *is* love. He could not not love. If he did not love, he would not be Father.

"My Chosen One in Whom I Delight"

Now, God could not *be* love if there were nobody to love. He could not be a Father without a child. And yet it is not as if God created *so that* he could love someone. He *is* love, and does not need to create in order to be who he is. If he did, what a needy, lonely thing he would be! "Poor old God," we'd say. If he created us in order to be who he is, *we* would be giving *him* life.

No, "Father," says Jesus the Son in John 17:24, "you loved *me* before the creation of the world." The eternal Son, who according to Colossians 1 is "before all things" (Col 1:17), the one through whom "all things were created" (Col 1:16), the one Hebrews 1 calls

"Lord" and "God," who "laid the foundations of the earth" (Heb 1:10)—it is he who is loved by the Father before the creation of the world. The Father, then, is the Father of the eternal Son, and he finds his very identity, his Fatherhood, in loving and giving out his life and being to the Son.

That is why it is important to note that the Son is the *eternal* Son. There was never a time when he didn't exist. If there were, then God is a completely different sort of being. If there were once a time when the Son didn't exist, then there was once a time when the Father was not yet a Father. And if that is the case, then once upon a time God was not loving since all by himself he would have had nobody to love. Commenting on Hebrews 1:3, which says that the Son is "the radiance of God's glory and the exact representation of his being," the fourth-century theologian Gregory of Nyssa explained that:

> As the light from the lamp is of the nature of that which sheds the brightness, and is united with it (for as soon as the lamp appears the light that comes from it shines out simultaneously), so in this place the Apostle would have us consider both that the Son is of the Father, and that the Father is never without the Son; for it is impossible that glory should be without radiance, as it is impossible that the lamp should be without brightness.[3]

The Father is never without the Son but, like a lamp, it is the very nature of the Father to shine out his Son. And likewise, it is the very nature of the Son to be the one who shines out from his Father. The Son has his very being from the Father. In fact, he *is* the going out—the radiance—of the Father's own being. He is the Son.

In all this we have been seeing that the Father loves and delights in the Son. That is what you see over and over again in Scripture: "The Father loves the Son and has placed everything in

---

[3]Gregory of Nyssa, in *Nicene and Post-Nicene Fathers,* ed. R. Schaff et al. (Buffalo, N.Y.: Christian Literature, 1887-1894), 2/5:338.

his hands" (Jn 3:35); "the Father loves the Son and shows him all
he does" (Jn 5:20), and so on (see also Is 42:1). But Jesus also says,
"the world must learn that *I love the Father* and that I do exactly
what my Father has commanded me" (Jn 14:31). So it is not just
that the Father loves the Son; the Son also loves the Father—and
so much so that to do his Father's pleasure is as food to him (Jn
4:34). It is his sheer joy and delight always to do as his Father says.

And yet, while the Father loves the Son and the Son loves the
Father, there is a very definite shape to their relationship. Overall,
the Father is the lover, the Son is the beloved. The Bible is awash
with talk of the Father's love for the Son, but while the Son clearly
does love the Father, hardly anything is said about it. The Father's
love is primary. The Father is the loving head. That then means
that in his love he will send and direct the Son, whereas the Son
never sends or directs the Father.

That turns out to be hugely significant, as the apostle Paul ob-
serves in 1 Corinthians 11:3: "Now I want you to realize that *the
head* of every man is Christ, and *the head* of the woman is man,
and *the head* of Christ is God." In other words, the shape of the
Father-Son relationship (the headship) begins a gracious cascade,
like a waterfall of love: as the Father is the lover and the head of
the Son, so the Son goes out to be the lover and the head of the
church. "As the Father has loved me, so have I loved you," the Son
says (Jn 15:9). And therein lies the very goodness of the gospel: as
the Father is the lover and the Son the beloved, so Christ becomes
the lover and the church the beloved. That means that Christ loves
the church first and foremost: his love is *not* a response, given only
when the church loves him; his love comes first, and we only love
him because he first loved us (1 Jn 4:19).

That dynamic is also to be replicated in marriages, husbands
being the heads of their wives, loving them as Christ the Head
loves his bride, the church. He is the lover, she is the beloved. Like
the church, then, wives are not left to earn the love of their hus-

bands; they can enjoy it as something lavished on them freely, unconditionally and maximally. For eternity, the Father so loves the Son that he excites the Son's eternal love in response; Christ so loves the church that he excites our love in response; the husband so loves his wife that he excites her to love him back. Such is the spreading goodness that rolls out of the very being of this God.

The Spirit of Love

The Father loves his Son in a very particular way, something we can see if we look at the baptism of Jesus: "As soon as Jesus was baptized, he went up out of the water. At that moment heaven was opened, and he saw the Spirit of God descending like a dove and lighting on him. And a voice from heaven said, 'This is my Son, whom I love; with him I am well pleased'" (Mt 3:16-17).

The Baptism of Christ by Master E. S. (1450)

Here, the Father declares his love for his Son, and his pleasure in him, and he does so *as the Spirit rests on Jesus.* For the way the Father makes known his love is precisely through giving his Spirit. In Romans 5:5, for instance, Paul writes of how God pours his love into our hearts *by the Holy Spirit.* It is, then, through giving him the Spirit that the Father declares his love for the Son.

It is all deeply personal: the Spirit stirs up the delight of the Father in the Son and the delight of the Son in the Father, inflaming their love and so binding them together in "the fellowship of the Holy Spirit" (2 Cor 13:14). He makes the Father's love known to the Son, causing him to cry "Abba!"—something he will also do for us (Rom 8:15; Gal 4:6). And let's be clear that "Abba!" is said with joy, for the Spirit so makes the Father known to the Son that the Son rejoices. "At that time Jesus, full of joy through the Holy Spirit, said, 'I praise you, Father, Lord of heaven and earth'" (Lk 10:21). For in making the loving Father of lights known, the Spirit is the bringer not only of love but of joy and is regularly associated with a joy next to which the merriness of wine is no substitute (Eph 5:18; see also Gal 5:22; Rom 14:17).

The way the Father, Son and Spirit related at Jesus' baptism was not a one-time-only event; the whole scene is full of echoes of Genesis 1. There at creation, the Spirit also hovered, dovelike, over waters. And just as the Spirit, after Jesus' baptism, would send him out into the lifeless wilderness, so in Genesis 1 the Spirit appears as the power by which God's Word goes out into the lifeless void. In the very beginning, God creates by his Word (the Word that would later become flesh), and he does so by sending out his Word in the power of his Spirit or Breath.

In both the work of creation (in Genesis 1) and the work of salvation or re-creation (in the Gospels), God's Word goes out from him by his Spirit. The Father speaks, and on his Breath his Word is heard. It all reveals what this God is truly like. The Spirit is the one through whom the Father loves, blesses and empowers his Son. The Son goes out from the Father by the Spirit. Hence Jesus is known as "the Anointed One" ("the Messiah" in Hebrew, "the Christ" in Greek), for he is the one supremely anointed with the Spirit. As kings and priests—even prophets—were anointed and consecrated to their tasks with oil in the Old Testament, Jesus is anointed with the Spirit. Indeed, the terms *Son* and *Anointed One* are sometimes almost synonymous (in, for example, Psalm 2).

The Father loves (and empowers) the Son by giving him his Spirit; that does not mean, though, that the Spirit is merely an impersonal divine force. Not at all. One could as well say the Son

THE GOD WHO SHARES

Sometime in the 1150s, a young Scot named Richard entered the Abbey of St. Victor, just outside the walls of Paris on the bank of the Seine. There he dedicated himself to contemplating God and was soon known as one of the most influential authors of his day.

Richard argued that if God were just one person, he could not be intrinsically loving, since for all eternity (before creation) he would have had nobody to love. If there were two persons, he went on, God might be loving, but in an excluding, ungenerous way. After all, when two persons love each other, they can be so infatuated with each other that they simply ignore everyone else—and a God like that would be very far from good news. But when the love between two persons is happy, healthy and secure, they rejoice to share it. Just so it is with God, said Richard. Being perfectly loving, from all eternity the Father and the Son have delighted to share their love and joy with and through the Spirit.

Richard of St. Victor (died 1173)

It is not, then, that God *becomes* sharing; being triune, God *is* a sharing God, a God who loves to include. Indeed, that is why God will go on to create. His love is not for keeping but for spreading.

is an impersonal force because of how he is called God's Word. In fact, the Son has many other titles which could make him sound equally impersonal ("the arm of the Lord," for instance, Is 53:1); but the point of such titles is to explain his role in each situation (as the Word he reveals God's mind, as the arm of the Lord he carries out his will); they do not suggest that the Son is in any way less than fully personal. And so it is with the Spirit: as a person he speaks and sends (Acts 13:2, 4); he chooses (Acts 20:28), teaches (Jn 14:26), gives (Is 63:14); he can be lied to and tested (Acts 5:3, 9); he can be resisted (Acts 7:51), grieved (Is 63:10; Eph 4:30) and blasphemed (Mt 12:31). In every way he is presented alongside the Father and the Son as a real person. When he is spoken of in the same breath as them (as when, for example, in Matthew 28:19, Jesus commands his disciples to go and make disciples, baptizing them in the name of the Father and of the Son and of the Holy Spirit), one has as much reason to think that the Father and the Son are impersonal as to think that the Spirit is.

A Heavenly Hodgepodge?

We are seeing that with this God we are dealing with three real and distinct persons, the Father, the Son and the Spirit. And they must be real persons: there could be no true love between them if they were, say, just different aspects of one single divine personality. Yet keeping them distinct in our minds is clearly a struggle: think how many times you have heard (or prayed): "Dear Father . . . thank you for dying for us"; "Dear Jesus . . . thank you for sending your Son. We pray this in Jesus' name," and so on.

Throwing the Father, Son and Spirit into a blender like this is politely called *modalism* by theologians. I prefer to call it *moodalism*. Moodalists think that God is one person who has three different moods (or modes, if you must). One popular moodalist idea is that God used to feel Fatherly (in the Old Testament), tried adopting a more Sonny disposition for thirty-some years, and has since decided to become more Spiritual. You understand the attraction, of course: it keeps things from becoming too complicated.

The trouble is, once you purée the persons, it becomes impossible to taste their gospel. If the Son is just a mood God slips in and out of, then for us to be adopted as children in the Son is no great thing: when God moves on to another mood, there will be no Son for us to be in. And even when God is in his Son mood, there will be no Father for us to be children of. And if the Spirit is just another of his states of mind, I can only wonder what will happen when God feels like moving on. "He fills me . . . he fills me not. . . ." The moodalist is left with no assurance and a deeply confused God. Somehow the Son must be his own Father, send himself, love himself, pray to himself, seat himself at his own right hand and so on. It all begins to look, dare I say, rather silly.

A Gaggle of Gods?

How, then, are we to take seriously the fact that the Father, Son and Spirit are three real and distinct persons, and not just three divine moods? The worry, of course, is that the Trinity could sound like some pantheon or club which divine persons can choose to join. As cows get together in herds and sheep in flocks, so divine persons congregate in the Trinity. And if that is it, then the Trinity begins to look much as Mount Olympus would have to the ancient Greeks—as Zeus, Apollo and the rest chose to cohabit there, so the Father, Son and Spirit assemble in the Trinity.

Now, because the Father, Son and Spirit are persons who have real relationships with each other (the Father loving the Son and so on), Christian theologians have happily and unabashedly spoken of the fellowship of the Trinity. The eighteenth-century theologian Jonathan Edwards could write about "the society or family of the three," even going so far as to say that the very "happiness of the Deity, as all other true happiness, consists in love and society."[4] But (and this is a big but) that is not to say that the Trinity is like a club that the Father, Son and Spirit have decided

---

[4]Jonathan Edwards, "Writings on the Trinity, Grace, and Faith," in *The Works of Jonathan Edwards,* ed. Sang Hyun Lee (New Haven and London: Yale University Press, 1957-2008), 21:135, 187.

to join. They are not three persons who simply manage to get along well—even very well—with each other.

What then? Well, let us go back to the beginning, and to the Father. Before creation, before all things, we saw, the Father was loving and begetting his Son. For eternity, that was what the Father was doing. He did not *become* Father at some point; rather, his very identity is to be the one who begets the Son. That is who he is. Thus it is not as if the Father and the Son bumped into each other at some point and found to their surprise how remarkably well they got on. The Father is who he is by virtue of his relationship with the Son. Think again of the image of the fountain: a fountain is not a fountain if it does not pour forth water. Just so, the Father would not be the Father without his Son (whom he loves through the Spirit). And the Son would not be the Son without his Father. He has his very being from the Father. And so we see that the Father, Son and Spirit, while distinct persons, are absolutely inseparable from each other. Not confused, but undividable. They are who they are *together*. They always *are* together, and thus they always *work* together.

That means that the Father is not "more" God than the Son or the Spirit, as if he had once existed or could exist without them. His very identity and being is about giving out his own fullness to the Son. He is inseparable from him. It also means there is no "God" behind and before Father, Son and Spirit. That, actually, can be the problem with talk about "God": it can all too easily lead us to imagine that there is some stuff (or worse, some person) called "God" out of which the Father, Son and Spirit then emerge. As if one could pray to this "God." As if anyone had ever met or had dealings with such a thing. Take even this traditional teaching aid, for example, sometimes called "The Shield of the Trinity": completely unintentionally, it can leave the impression that there is in the middle some fourth thing called "God" beside the Father, Son and Spirit. If that were the case, of course, then not only would there be four in the Trinity; but also, Father, Son and Spirit really would be different gods, each just consisting of the same "stuff." But starting with the Father we avoid all such nastiness: behind everything, instead of some abstract "God," we see the Father, whose nature it is to give himself and beget his Son.

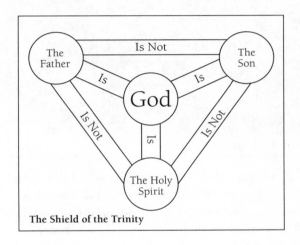

The Shield of the Trinity

Eggs and Shamrocks Redux

Now come back to those "illustrations" of the Trinity: the three states of H_2O and all that. How do they seem? Is the triune God like H_2O, the Father all icy until you warm him up and he turns into the watery Son, who then vaporizes and becomes the steamy Spirit when you really crank up the heat? No, that's just modalism. Is God like a shamrock leaf, the Father, Son and Spirit just three bits sticking out? One can hear the whine as old Hilarius starts to do a steady 90 rpm in his grave. Quite apart from anything else, such pictures make God out to be an impersonal *thing*. Not personal, not loving—not like the Father, Son and Spirit at all.

If the Bible ever comes out with an image, it is in Genesis 1 and 2.

Then God said, "Let *us* make man in *our* image, in *our* likeness, and let them rule over the fish of the sea and the

ST. HILARIUS

St. Hilarius (300?-367?)

Cheerful by name, cheerful by theology: that was Hilarius. (Today he is ponderously styled "Hilary of Poitiers," but that only shows what a sad state we are in.) With wits like a rapier and manners like a lamb, he gave his life and liberty to defend the Son's eternal deity. He argued powerfully that the followers of Arius, who held that the Son had begun to exist at some point, were making a disastrous mistake: saying that there had not always been a Son meant that God had not always been a Father. Thus God is not fundamentally a Father, not essentially loving and life-giving, but something else.

But Hilarius refused absolutely to believe in "a certain imaginary substance" from which the Father and the Son might have come. Underneath everything there is not "God," but the Father, eternally loving his Son. "God," he said, "can never be anything but love, or anything but the Father: and He, Who loves, does not envy; He Who is Father, is wholly and entirely Father. This name admits of no compromise: no one can be partly father, and partly not." In other words, there is no cold, abstract "God" or "God-stuff" behind Father, Son and Spirit. At bottom there is the Father, and that means a lively God of love, a God who is no envious, life-hoarding miser, but who delights to give out his life and being to his Son.

To stop people thinking that there might be any "God" behind the Father, Son and Spirit, Hilarius advised: "We must confess Father and Son before we can apprehend God as One and true."[a] Trying to define God without starting with the Father and his Son, he saw, one would quite simply wind up with a different God.

[a]Hilarius, *On the Trinity* 4.4; 9.61; 5.35.

birds of the air, over the livestock, over all the earth, and over all the creatures that move along the ground." So God created man in his own image, in the image of God he created him; *male and female* he created them. (Gen 1:26-27)

There is something about the relationship and difference between the man and the woman, Adam and Eve, that images the being of God—something we saw the apostle Paul pick up on in 1 Corinthians 11:3. Eve is a person quite distinct from Adam, and yet she has all her life and being from Adam. She comes from his side, is bone of his bones and flesh of his flesh, and is one with him in the flesh (Gen 2:21-24). Far better than leaves, eggs and liquids, that reflects a personal God, a Son who is distinct from his Father, and yet who is of the very being of the Father, and who is eternally one with him in the Spirit.

Mere Trinitarianism

John wrote his gospel, he tells us, so "that you may believe that Jesus is the Christ, the Son of God, and that by believing you may have life in his name" (Jn 20:31). But even that most basic call to believe in the Son of God is an invitation to a Trinitarian faith. Jesus is described as the *Son* of God. God is his Father. And he is the Christ, the one anointed with the Spirit. When you start with the Jesus of the Bible, it is a triune God that you get. The Trinity, then, is not the product of abstract speculation: when you proclaim Jesus, the Spirit-anointed Son of the Father, you proclaim the triune God.

And what Arius demonstrated was the reverse: when you *don't* start with Jesus the Son, you end up with a different God who is not the Father. For the Son is the one Way to know God truly: only he reveals the Father. John Calvin once wrote that if we try to think about God without thinking about the Father, Son and Spirit, then "only the bare and empty name of God flits about in our brains, to the exclusion of the true God."[5] He was quite right. For there is a vast world of difference between the triune God revealed by Jesus and all other gods.

This God simply will not fit into the mold of any other. For the Trinity is not some inessential add-on to God, some optional software that can be plugged into him. At bottom this God is different, for at bottom, he is not Creator, Ruler or even "God" in some abstract sense: he is the Father, loving and giving life to his Son in the fellowship of the Spirit. A God who is in himself love, who before all things could "never be anything but love." Having such a God happily changes everything.

---

[5]Calvin, *Institutes* 1.13.2.

2

Creation

THE FATHER'S LOVE OVERFLOWS

Single God, Nonsmoker, Seeks Attractive Creation with Good Sense of Humor . . .

Imagine for a moment that you are God. I'm sure you've done it before. Now think: Would you in your divine wisdom and power ever want to create a universe and, if so, why? Because you feel lonely and want some friends? Because you like being pampered and want some servants? It is one of the profoundest questions to ask: If there is a God, why is there anything else? Why the universe? Why us? Why might God decide to have a creation?

Marduk with his pet dragon

One of the earliest attempts at an answer can be seen in ancient Babylon's creation myth, the *Enuma Elish*. There the god Marduk puts it bluntly: he will create humankind so that the gods can have slaves. That way the gods can sit back and live off the labor of their human workforce. Now Marduk is more plain-speaking than most other gods, but whatever the religion, most gods since have tended to like his approach. And who can blame them? His reasoning is profoundly attractive. If you are a god.

In fact, the reason most gods follow Marduk's lead is not just a matter of personal preference. Imagine a god who is the origin and cause of everything else. He brought everyone and everything into being. Now before he caused anything else to exist, this god was all alone. He had not made anyone yet. Solitary for eternity, then. And so, for eternity this solitary god can have had nobody and nothing to love. Love for others is clearly not his heartbeat. Of course he would probably love himself, but such love we tend to think of as selfish and not truly *loving*. By his very nature, therefore, this lonely, single god must be fundamentally inward-looking and not outgoingly loving. Essentially, he is all about private self-gratification. That, therefore, is the only reason why he would create.

There is a fascinating tension at just this point in Islam. Traditionally, Allah is said to have ninety-nine names, titles which describe him as he is in himself in eternity. One of them is "The Loving." But how could Allah be loving in eternity? Before he created there was nothing else in existence that he could love (and the title does not refer to self-centered love but love for others). The only option is that Allah eternally loves his creation. But that in itself raises an enormous problem: if Allah needs his creation to be who he is in himself ("loving"), then Allah is dependent on his own creation, and one of the cardinal beliefs of Islam is that Allah is dependent on nothing.

Therein lies the problem: how can a solitary God be eternally and essentially loving when love involves loving another? In the fourth century B.C., the Athenian philosopher Aristotle wrestled with a very similar question: how can God be eternally and essentially good when goodness involves being good *to another*? His answer was that God *is*, eternally, the uncaused cause. That is who God is. Therefore he must eternally cause the creation to exist, meaning that the universe is eternal. This way God can be truly and eternally good, for the universe eternally exists alongside him and

eternally he gives his goodness
to it. In other words, God is
eternally self-giving and good
because he is eternally self-
giving and good *to the universe.*
It was, as always with Aristotle,
ingenious. However, once again
it means that for God to be
himself, he needs the world. He
is, essentially, dependent on it
to be who he is. And, even
though technically "good," Aristotle's god is hardly kind or
loving. He does not freely

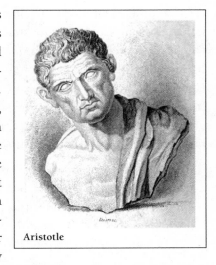

Aristotle

choose to create a world that he might bless; it is more that the universe just oozes out of him.

Such are the problems with nontriune gods and creation.
Single-person gods, having spent eternity alone, are inevitably
self-centered beings, and so it becomes hard to see why they would
ever cause anything else to exist. Wouldn't the existence of a universe be an irritating distraction for the god whose greatest
pleasure is looking in a mirror? Creating just looks like a deeply
unnatural thing for such a god to do. And if such gods do create,
they always seem to do so out of an essential neediness or desire
to *use* what they create merely for their own self-gratification.

God's Ecstasy

Everything changes when it comes to the Father, Son and Spirit.
Here is a God who is not essentially lonely, but who has been
loving for all eternity as the Father has loved the Son in the Spirit.
Loving others is not a strange or novel thing for this God at all; it
is at the root of who he is.

Think of God the Father: he is, by his very nature, life-giving.

He is a father. One has to wonder if a barren god, who is not a father, is capable of giving life and so birthing a creation. But one can have no such doubts with the Father: for eternity he has been fruitful, potent, vitalizing. For such a God (and only for such a God) it seems very natural and entirely unsurprising that he should bring about more life and so create.

Karl Barth made a profound (but densely stated!) observation here that we will try to unpack:

> In the same freedom and love in which God is not alone in Himself but is the eternal begetter of the Son, who is the eternally begotten of the Father, He also turns as Creator *ad extra* [outward] in order that absolutely and outwardly He may not be alone but the One who loves in freedom. In other words, as God in Himself is neither deaf nor dumb but speaks and hears His Word from all eternity, so outside His eternity He does not wish to be without hearing or echo, that is, without the ears and voices of the creature. The eternal fellowship between Father and Son, or between God and His Word, thus finds a correspondence in the very different but not dissimilar fellowship between God and His creature. It is in keeping with the Father of the eternal Son, the One who speaks the eternal Word as such; it is wholly worthy of Him, that in His dealings *ad extra* [outward] He should be the Creator.[1]

Yes, theologians often write like that. What he means is that, since God the Father has eternally loved his Son, it is entirely characteristic of him to turn and create others that he might also love them. Now Barth is absolutely not saying that God the Son was created or is in any way less than fully God. It is that the Father has always enjoyed loving *another,* and so the act of creation by which he creates others to love seems utterly appropriate for him.

---

[1]Karl Barth, *Church Dogmatics* III/1, ed. G. W. Bromiley and T. F. Torrance (Edinburgh: T & T Clark, 1936-1977), p. 50.

Thus Jesus Christ, God the Son, is the Logic, the blueprint for creation. He is the one eternally loved by the Father; creation is about the extension of that love outward so that it might be enjoyed by others. The fountain of love brimmed over. The Father so delighted in his Son that his love for him overflowed, so that the Son might be the firstborn among many sons. As Paul puts it in Romans 8:29, "For those God foreknew he also predestined to be conformed to the likeness of his Son, that he might be the firstborn among many brothers" (see also Eph 1:3-5). This God does not begrudge having someone else beside him: he enjoys it. He has always enjoyed showering his love on his Son, and in creating he rejoices to shower it on children he loves through the Son.

Interestingly, when Paul writes of the Son as "the firstborn over all creation" in Colossians, he directly connects that idea with the fact that the Son is "the image" of God. "He is the image of the invisible God, the firstborn over all creation" (Col 1:15). The Son is the image of God, perfectly showing us what his Father is like. "The Son is the radiance of God's glory and the exact representation of his being" (Heb 1:3; see also 2 Cor 4:4). And so, as he gloriously goes, "shines" and "radiates" out from his Father, he shows us that the Father is essentially *outgoing*. It is unsurprising that such a God should create. And that we should then be created in the image of God and destined to be conformed into the likeness of Christ the Image is simply the continuation of that outgoing movement of love. The God who loves to have an outgoing Image of himself in his Son loves to have many images of his love (who are themselves outgoing).

There is something Jesus says at the end of his high priestly prayer in John 17 that shows clearly what it means for him to be the glory of God who shines out from his Father (or the Word of God who goes out from God):

> Father, I want those you have given me to be with me where
> I am, and to see my glory, the glory you have given me be-

cause *you loved me before the creation of the world.* Righteous
Father, though the world does not know you, I know you,
and they know that you have sent me. I have made you
known to them, and will continue to make you known in
order *that the love you have for me may be in them* and that I
myself may be in them. (Jn 17:24-26)

The Father loved him before the creation of the world, and the
reason the Father sends him is so that the Father's love for him
might be in others also. That is why the Son goes out from the
Father, in both creation and salvation: that the love of the Father
for the Son might be shared.

Because in a sense the Son is the model for creation, his response to the Father also serves as the model for how creation and
all creatures should themselves respond. Jesus said that "the world
must learn that I love the Father" (Jn 14:31). And so, just as the
Father decided to include us in his love for the Son, to share it
with us, so the Son chose to include us in his love for the Father.
He delights to echo his Father's love back to him, and that is what
it is to be beside God, to image him, to be his child. We have been
created that, knowing his love, we might love the Lord our God.

All this is to say that the very nature of the triune God is at complete odds with the nature of other gods. In *The Screwtape Letters,*
C. S. Lewis captured well the difference between the devil (who is
the definitive needy and solitary god) and the living God of ecstatic,
self-giving, overflowing love. Screwtape, a senior demon, writes:

One must face the fact that all the talk about His love for
men, and His service being perfect freedom, is not (as one
would gladly believe) mere propaganda, but an appalling
truth. He really *does* want to fill the universe with a lot of
loathsome little replicas of Himself—creatures, whose life,
on its miniature scale, will be qualitatively like His own, not
because He has absorbed them but because their wills freely

conform to His. We want cattle who can finally become food; He wants servants who can finally become sons. We want to suck in, He wants to give out. We are empty and would be filled; He is full and flows over.[2]

IT'S ALL GREEK TO ME

There are two Greek words you will never use on a holiday in Corfu, but they drip with nectar. The first is *hypostasis*. I know, it sounds like a nasty skin condition, but it actually means something like "foundation" (*hypo* = "under"; *stasis* = "something which stands or exists"). The Greek Old Testament uses the word in Psalm 69:2 when the psalmist says, "I sink in the miry depths, where there is no *foothold [hypostasis]*." In other words, there is nothing firm underneath for him to stand on. But it is also the word used to describe God's "being" in Hebrews 1:3 ("The Son is the radiance of God's glory and the exact representation of his *being [hypostasis]*"). Hypostasis describes the Father's "being," what is foundational to him.[a]

The other word is *ekstasis,* from which we get the word *ecstasy*. It is a word to do with being beside yourself or being outside yourself (*ek* = "out from"; *stasis* = "something which stands or exists").

What we have been seeing is that the Father, Son and Spirit have their *hypostasis* in *ekstasis*. That is, God's innermost being *(hypostasis)* is an outgoing, loving, life-giving being. The triune God is an *ecstatic* God: he is not a God who hoards his life, but one who gives it away, as he would show in that supreme moment of his self-revelation on the cross. The Father finds his very identity in giving his life and being to the Son; and the Son images his Father in sharing his life with us through the Spirit.

[a]Theologians would come to speak of the Father, Son and Spirit each being a *hypostasis*. What they meant by this is vital: that there is nothing more foundational in God than the Father, Son and Spirit. There is no "God" or "God-stuff" behind them or from which they emerge.

[2]C. S. Lewis, *The Screwtape Letters* (Glasgow: Collins, 1942), pp. 45-46.

Hell as a monstrous, ravenous mouth by the
Master of Catherine of Cleves

And Screwtape is not alone: he seems to think in remarkably
similar ways to Artemis of the Ephesians. In Acts 19, Demetrius
the idol-maker complains that if Paul is allowed to say that "man-
made gods are no gods at all," then

> "there is danger not only that our trade will lose its good
> name, but also that the temple of the great goddess Artemis
> will be discredited, and the goddess herself, who is wor-
> shiped throughout the province of Asia and the world, will
> be robbed of her divine majesty." When they heard this, they
> were furious and began shouting: "Great is Artemis of the
> Ephesians!" (Acts 19:27-28)

In other words, the divine majesty of Artemis is dependent on
the service of her worshipers. In herself she sounds empty and
parasitic, as if her magnificence is nothing but the glisten of the
silver brought to her temple by her minions.

The tragedy is that so many think that the living God is the
devilish one here, as if he created us simply to get, to demand, to
take from us. But the contrast between the devil and the triune

God could hardly be starker: the first is empty, hungry, grasping, envious; the second is superabundant, generous, radiant and self-giving.[3] And *thus* the triune God can and does create. Grace, then, is not merely his kindness to those who have sinned; the very creation is a work of grace, flowing from God's love. Love is not a mere reaction with this God. In fact, it is not a reaction at all. God's love is creative. *Love comes first.* He gives life and being as a free gift, for his very life, being and goodness is yeasty, spreading out that there might be more that is truly good.

The eighteenth-century New England theologian Jonathan Edwards put it strikingly. God's aim in creating the world, he said, *was* himself. But because this God's very *self* is so different from that of any others, that means something utterly different from what it would mean with other gods. This God's very self is found in giving, not taking. This God is like a fountain of goodness, and so, he said, "seeking himself" *means* seeking "himself diffused and expressed"—in other words, seeking to have himself, his life and his goodness shared.[4] His very nature is about going out and sharing of his own fullness, and so that is what he is all about. In contrast to all other gods, the exuberant nature of this God means that his pleasure "is rather a pleasure in diffusing and communicating to the creature, than in receiving from the creature."[5]

How Did the Triune God Create?

Because it is the Father's love for the Son that is the motive behind creation, the Nicene Creed ascribes creation especially to the Father: "We believe in one God, the Father Almighty, Maker of

---

[3]As an example of the contrast, compare how in 1 Peter 5 God is spoken of in verse 7 and the devil is spoken of in verse 8. We can cast all our anxiety on God because he cares for us (1 Pet 5:7), whereas the devil is looking for someone to devour (1 Pet 5:8).
[4]Jonathan Edwards, "Ethical Writings," in *The Works of Jonathan Edwards,* ed. Paul Ramsey (New Haven and London: Yale University Press, 1957-2008), 8:459.
[5]Ibid., p. 448.

IN THE SUNSHINE OF GOD'S LOVE

People usually think of "the Puritans" as a pinched and frost-bitten lot: sour, picky and, bluntly, so boring that pigeons could roost on them. Well, some of them were.

But not Richard Sibbes. Sibbes, a rough contemporary of Shakespeare, was a Puritan preacher and theologian who spoke so winningly of the kindness and love of God that he came to be known as "the honey-mouthed" preacher. Yet it was not simply that Sibbes was born with a sunny disposition; he himself was adamant that it is our view of God that shapes us most deeply. We become like what we worship.[a]

Richard Sibbes (1577-1635)

And Sibbes clearly saw the triune God as winning, kind and lovely: he spoke of the living God as a life-giving, warming sun who "delights to spread his beams and his influence in inferior things, to make all things fruitful. Such a goodness is in God as is in a fountain, or in the breast that loves to ease itself of milk."[a] That is, God is simply bursting with warm and life-imparting nourishment, far more willing to give than we are to receive. And that, he explained, is precisely why he created the world:

> If God had not a communicative, spreading goodness, he would never have created the world. The Father, Son, and Holy Ghost were happy in themselves, and enjoyed one another before the world was. Apart from the fact that God delights to communicate and spread his goodness, there had never been a creation or redemption.[b]

It is not, then, that God *needed* to create the world in order to satisfy himself or to be himself. The divine majesty of this God is not dependent on the world. The Father, Son and Spirit "were happy in themselves, and enjoyed one another before the world was." But the Father so enjoyed his fellowship with his Son that he wanted to have the goodness of it spread out and communicated or shared with others. The creation was a free choice borne out of nothing but love.

It was the knowledge that God is so sunny, so radiant with goodness and love, that made Sibbes such an attractive model of Godlikeness. For, he said, "those that are led with the Spirit of God, that are like him; they have a communicative, diffusive goodness that loves to spread itself."[c] In other words, knowing God's love, he became loving; and his understanding of who God is transformed him into a man, a preacher and a writer of magnetic geniality. That amiability shone through his preaching; it still glows from his writings; and looking at his life, it is clear that he had a quite extraordinary ability for cultivating warm and lasting friendships. He had become like his God.

---

[a]Richard Sibbes, "The Successful Seeker," in *Works of Richard Sibbes* (Edinburgh: James Nichol, 1862-64), 6:113.
[b]Ibid.
[c]Ibid.

---

heaven and earth." Flowing from his love, it is his to command into being. Thus the cry in Revelation 4:11 goes up specifically to him: "You are worthy, our Lord and God, to receive glory and honor and power, for you created all things, and by your will they were created and have their being."

But, as can be seen in Genesis 1, he creates through his Word and his Spirit. One second-century theologian, Irenaeus of Lyons, therefore liked to speak of the Son and the Spirit as the Father's "two hands." He did not at all mean to imply that the Son and the Spirit are not really persons (Jesus himself was prepared to speak of the Spirit as the "finger of God": compare Mt 12:28/Lk 11:20); it is that the Son and the Spirit are the Father's agents, bringing about the will of the Father.

The roles the Son and the Spirit have in creation are rather different, though. As we saw in the last chapter, in Genesis 1 the Word goes out in the power of the hovering Spirit so that on God's Breath his Word is heard: "Let there be light!" Thus the Father creates *through* his Word (Jn 1:3), the Word being his executive arm. This means that the Son is so fully involved in his Father's work of creation that Paul can write: "He is the image of the invisible God, the firstborn over all creation. For by him all things were created: things in heaven and on earth, visible and invisible, whether thrones or powers or rulers or authorities; all things were created by him and for him" (Col 1:15-16).

"And for him." It was his overflowing love for the Son that motivated the Father to create, and creation is his gift to his Son. The Father makes his Son the inheritor, the "heir of all things" (Heb 1:2; but see also Deut 32:8-9; Ps 2:8). And so the Son is not only the motivating origin of creation: he is its goal. The Son is the Alpha and the Omega, the beginning and the end of creation. Now here we come to something astounding: because the Father's love for the Son has burst out to be shared with us, the Son's inheritance is also (extraordinarily!) shared with us. "Now if we are children, then we are heirs—heirs of God and co-heirs with Christ" (Rom 8:17). It is a physical expression of the marvelous truth that the Father shares his love of the Son with us: the meek shall inherit the earth!

Alpha and Omega

So, some Scriptures speak of creation as the work of the Father (it is conceived in his love); others speak of creation as the work of the Son (he brings about his Father's will); but still others speak of it as the work of the Spirit. "By the word of the LORD were the heavens made, their starry host by the *breath* [or Spirit] of his mouth" (Ps 33:6). How? What is the

Spirit's role? We have already seen that the Spirit empowers the Word, but he does even more: while the Son establishes and upholds all things (Heb 1:3), the Spirit perfects or completes the work of creation. Job 26:13 puts it delightfully: "By his breath [or Spirit] the skies *became fair*." In other words, the Spirit garnishes and beautifies the heavens and the earth. Our first vision of the Spirit, hovering dovelike in Genesis 1, captures something essential. It is that, like a mothering dove settling on her eggs, the Spirit vivifies, bringing what has been created to life. And so, while the Nicene Creed speaks of the Father as the "Maker of heaven and earth," it speaks of the Spirit as "the Lord and giver of life."

Life is something that God has always had, and in creation it is something he now shares with us. By his Spirit he breathes out life on us. And not just in the beginning: that is always the Spirit's work, to bring life. In the book of Job, Elihu says, "The Spirit of God has made me; the breath of the Almighty gives me life" (Job 33:4). Ongoingly in his creation, the Spirit vitalizes and refreshes. He delights to make his creation—and his creatures—*fruitful*. Isaiah writes of the time when "the Spirit is poured upon us from on high, and the desert becomes a fertile field, and the fertile field seems like a forest" (Is 32:15). The psalmist sings: "When you send your Spirit, they [the creatures] are created, and you renew the face of the earth" (Ps 104:30). Small wonder, then, that creativity, the ability to craft, adorn and make beautiful, is a gift of the Spirit:

> Then the LORD said to Moses, "See, I have chosen Bezalel son of Uri, the son of Hur, of the tribe of Judah, and I have filled him with the Spirit of God, with skill, ability and knowledge in all kinds of crafts—to make artistic designs for work in gold, silver and bronze, to cut and set stones, to work in wood, and to engage in all kinds of craftsmanship." (Ex 31:1-5)

The Spirit makes his creation alive with beauty. Gerard Manley

Hopkins captured it finely when he wrote of the Spirit's work of freshening even a world now made weary with sin:

> There lives the dearest freshness deep down things;
> And though the last lights off the black West went
> Oh, morning, at the brown brink eastward, springs—
> Because the Holy Ghost over the bent
> World broods with warm breast and with ah! bright wings.[6]

"And It Was Good"

God the Father is a God who delights to have another beside him (his eternal Son). He is a God who thinks that is good. And thus he is a God who can declare his creation good. If he had been eternally alone, preoccupied only with himself, it is hard to believe he could do that. The new existence of something else beside him would surely be a nuisance, or perhaps appear to be a rival. Take, for example, something the enormously influential Muslim theologian Abu Hamid al-Ghazali (1056-1111) once wrote: "God does indeed love them [people], but in reality He loves nothing other than Himself, in the sense that He is the totality [of being], and there is nothing in being apart from Him."[7]

Because Allah really "loves nothing other than Himself," he does not really turn outward to express his love to others. Thus there can be no reason why anything else should exist. Really, therefore, "there is nothing in being apart from Him." Of course, the Qur'an speaks of Allah's love and of creation, but it is hard to see quite how those things can be. The universe, in Islamic thought, must have only a shadowy, uncertain existence.

And to look around, it certainly seems the case that absolutely singular supreme beings tend to show a marked awkwardness about the existence of creation. In such belief systems, the

---

[6]Gerard Manley Hopkins, "God's Grandeur," lines 10-14.
[7]Abu Hamid al-Ghazali, *The Revival of Religious Studies,* trans. Reza Shah-Kazemi (Louisville: Fons Vitae, 2002), 6.36.

physical is routinely viewed negatively and with caution. And the hope such gods offer does not usually include ever getting to see, know or relate to them. They offer "paradise," but will not really be there themselves. Why would they want to be involved with creation?

A stark example of this can be seen in a rather odd collection of second- and third-century beliefs we call Gnosticism. If you've read Dan Brown's *The Da Vinci Code,* or seen the film, you will have come across Gnosticism. In the world of Dan Brown, orthodox Christianity is an authoritarian, chauvinist, intolerant religion: that, apparently, is what the God of Christianity is like and so that is how his servants are. But on the sidelines of history, persecuted and chased into hiding, are the Gnostics; and in Dan Brown's mind, the Gnostics were the open-minded, tolerant, protofeminist goodies.

Well, now. Let us see. In Gnosticism, everything started with The One.[8] That is, there was a spiritual realm and nothing more. Everything was fine and divine. Imagine the room you are in now being that realm: in the room there is peace and a really good book you'd recommend to your friends. Outside the room, absolutely nothing exists. Then, somehow, something goes wrong. A disturbance in the room. The dog starts throwing up on the carpet, say. Of course, you want to keep reading the really good book, so the disturbance and its mess must be thrown out. But now, as soon as the disturbance is thrown out of the room, something troublesome and obnoxious exists outside the room. And that is Gnosticism's account of creation: once there was only the spiritual realm; something went wrong; the problem got thrown outside; now something exists outside the spiritual realm and that became the physical universe.

---

[8]To be fussy, "Gnosticism" was actually a grab-bag of disconnected little sects, so we can't really say what "Gnostics" believed, but the above is an attempt to outline what was at least pretty standard fare.

Where Genesis speaks of a good creation and *then* a fall into evil, Gnosticism imagined *first* a fall into evil, and creation as the result. For the Gnostics, the One was good; the existence of something else beside it is bad. Thus they could speak of that something else (the universe, our bodies and everything physical) being like noxious vomit spewed forth from the One. The good news, they held, was that, like a dog, the One would return to its vomit and suck it all back up. Then everything physical would be consumed and ingested by the spiritual, all would happily be just One again, and the universe would be but an embarrassing memory in the mind of the One.

Absolutely singular supreme beings do not like creation.

"IT IS NOT GOOD FOR THE MAN TO BE ALONE"

If that was how the Gnostics rearranged Genesis 1, inserting a "not" into every "God saw it was good," just imagine how they read Genesis 2 and the story of the creation of Eve. For them, the chapter starts quite positively: the man is alone. There is only one. That must be good. But then, horribly, and just as the physical realm was ex-

The Lord God taking Eve from Adam's side

creted from the spiritual, Eve comes out of Adam. Now there are two. And just as the existence of two realms (spiritual and physical) is bad, so the existence of two sexes is bad. More specifically, the existence of women is bad. Thus the final verse in the Gnostic *Gospel of Thomas* reads: "Simon Peter said to them, 'Let Mary leave us, for women are not worthy of life.' Jesus said, 'I myself shall lead her in order to make her male, so that she too may become a living spirit resembling you males. For every woman who will make herself male will enter the kingdom of heaven.'"[a]

That verse does not come across as jarring or awkward at the end of the *Gospel of Thomas;* it is the natural child of Gnostic thought. The existence of two realms, two sexes, of the physical and the feminine, is a tragedy. But such must be the case with a lonely and solitary supreme being. Intolerant of the existence of anything else, it is only natural that he should prefer to hide both the physical and the feminine away, or use them if he can only for his own self-gratification. And so for women at least, Gnostic salvation would mean gender-bending. Dan Brown's insinuation that the Gnostics were the tolerant protofeminists sounds very hollow indeed.

And those chauvinist Christians? Believing that God is not lonely, it made perfect sense to say that it is not good to have men alone. As God is not alone, so a human in his image should not be alone. They therefore upheld creation and the physical, femininity, relationship and marriage all as being intrinsically good, created reflections of a God who is not lonely.

Without the Trinity, it is hard to see how such things could be ultimately affirmed. (Of course, one could simply argue that men and women are equal because they are both human, but that is an entirely loveless affirmation, and gives no grounds for seeing those things as absolute goods to be reveled in.) The apostle Paul wrote in 1 Corinthians 11:3 that as the head of Christ is God, so the head of a wife is her husband. But if the Son is less God than his Father, is a wife less human than her husband? Without belief in God the Father and the Son, one in the Spirit, why should a husband not treat his wife as a lesser being? Yet if a husband's headship of his wife is somehow akin to the Father's headship of the Son, then what a loving relationship must ensue! The Father's very identity is about giving life, love and being to his Son, doing all out of love for him.

Of course, that is not to say that Christians have always got things right here or lived out these beliefs, but it does start to kick back strongly against the idea that Christianity is inherently chauvinist.

Belief in the Trinity works precisely *against* chauvinism and *for* delight in harmonious relationships.

And that told historically as Christianity first spread through the ancient Greco-Roman world. Studies have shown that in that world it was quite extraordinarily rare for even large families ever to have more than one daughter. How is that possible across countries and centuries? Quite simply because abortion and female infanticide were widely practiced so as to relieve families of the burden of a gender considered largely superfluous. No surprise, then, that Christianity should have been so especially attractive to women, who made up so many of the early converts: Christianity decried those life-threatening ancient abortion procedures; it refused to ignore the infidelity of husbands as paganism did; in Christianity, widows would be and were supported by the church; they were even welcomed as "fellow-workers" in the gospel (Rom 16:3). In Christianity, women were valued.

[a]*The Gospel of Thomas*, Logion 114, in J. M. Robinson, ed., *The Nag Hammadi Library*, 3rd ed. (San Francisco: Harper & Row, 1988), p. 139; see also Logion 22.

Explaining Good . . .

The very nature of the triune God is to be effusive, ebullient and bountiful; the Father rejoices to have another beside him, and he finds his very self in pouring out his love. Creation is about the spreading, the diffusion, the outward explosion of that love. This God is the very opposite of greedy, hungry, selfish emptiness; in his self-giving he naturally pours forth life and goodness. He is, then, the source of all that is good, and that means he is not the sort of God who would call people to himself away from happiness in good things. Goodness and ultimate happiness are to be found with him, not apart from him.

And the bountiful nature of the triune Creator makes all the difference to how we view the creation. If Marduk had had his way, and we existed to be slaves, the creation would simply provide the raw materials to keep the work-gang going. As it is, there is something gratuitous about creation, an unnecessary abundance of beauty, and through its blossoms and pleasures we can revel in the sheer largesse of the Father. In fact, said C. S. Lewis, even if our views of God prevent *us* from doing so, this is just what the animals do. Writing to his friend Owen Barfield shortly after World War II, he remarked:

> Talking of beasts and birds, have you ever noticed this contrast: that when you read a scientific account of any animal's life you get an impression of laborious, incessant, almost rational economic activity . . . but when you study any animal you know—what at once strikes you is their cheerful fatuity, the pointlessness of nearly all they do. Say what you like, Barfield, the world is sillier and better fun than they make out.[9]

It makes all the difference: is this world a desert of mere, grim survival—a workhouse for the gods—or is it the gift of the most kind and generous Father?

. . . And Evil

If God is not triune, it gets even worse: for if God is not triune, it becomes very difficult, not only to account for the goodness of creation (as we have seen), but also to account for the existence of evil within it. If God is the supreme being, then evil cannot be some rival force, eternally existing beside God. Yet if God is absolutely solitary in his supremacy, then surely evil must originate in God himself. Above and before all things, he is the source of all things, both good and evil. Clearly, it is not good for God to be alone.

The triune God, however, is the sort of God who will make room for another to have real existence. The Father, who delights

---

[9]C. S. Lewis, *Collected Letters: Books, Broadcasts, and War, 1931–1949,* ed. Walter Hooper (New York: HarperCollins, 2004), p. 930.

to have a Son, chooses to create many children who will have real lives of their own, to share the love and freedom he has always enjoyed. The creatures of the triune God are not mere extensions of him; he gives them life and personal being. Allowing them that, though, means allowing them to turn away from himself—and that is the origin of evil. By graciously giving his creatures the room to exist, the triune God allows them the freedom to turn away without himself being the author of evil.

From Harmony to Harmony

Christianity has always had a special love affair with music. The Scriptures are shot through with music, as is life in the church. John Dryden, the seventeenth-century poet, tried to explain why it should be so in his "A Song for St. Cecilia's Day" (Saint Cecilia is the patron saint of church music):

> From harmony, from Heav'nly harmony
> This universal frame began.
> When Nature underneath a heap
> Of jarring atoms lay,
> And could not heave her head,
> The tuneful voice was heard from high,
> "Arise ye more than dead!"
> Then cold, and hot, and moist, and dry,
> In order to their stations leap,
> And music's pow'r obey.
> From harmony, from Heav'nly harmony
> This universal frame began:
> From harmony to harmony
> Through all the compass of the notes it ran,
> The diapason [octave] closing full in man.

Dryden's words find echoes throughout the Christian world: C. S. Lewis had the Christlike figure of Aslan sing Narnia into existence in *The Magician's Nephew;* his friend J. R. R. Tolkien imagined the creation of the cosmos as a musical event in *The Silmarillion;* and in the eighteenth century, George Frideric Handel set Dryden's ode to music so you can actually hear melodically how, after a dramatic silence and void that reminds one of Genesis 1, the overflowing joy of the heavenly harmony bursts out.

It is from the heavenly harmony of Father, Son and Spirit that this universal frame of the cosmos—and all created harmony—comes. To hear a tuneful harmony can be one of the most intoxicatingly beautiful experiences. And no wonder: as in heaven, so on earth. The Father, Son and Spirit have always been in delicious harmony, and thus they create a world where harmonies—distinct beings, persons or notes working in unity—are good, mirroring the very being of the triune God.

The eternal harmony of the Father, Son and Spirit provides the logic for a world in which everything was created to exist in cheerful conviviality, and which still, despite the discord of sin and evil, is so essentially harmonious. The fourth-century theologian Athanasius thus compared God the Son to a musician, and the universe to his lyre:

> Just as though some musician, having tuned a lyre, and by his art adjusted the high notes to the low, and the intermediate notes to the rest, were to produce a single tune as the result, so also the Wisdom of God, handling the Universe as a lyre, and adjusting things in the air to things on the earth, and things in the heaven to things in the air, and combining parts into wholes and moving them all by His beck and will, produces well and fittingly, as the result, the unity of the universe and of its order.[10]

And such thoughts have inspired many a Christian musician.

---

[10]Athanasius, *Against the Heathen* 42.

Johann Sebastian Bach (1685-1750)

Johann Sebastian Bach, for instance, was deeply committed to the idea that the human musician could echo and sound out the cosmic harmony of the divine musician; the orderliness, the minor and the major keys, the shadows and the lights in the music all resonating the structure of the great symphony that is creation. In writing such music, Bach quite deliberately sought to provide fuel for both mind and heart, challenging the intellect and stirring the affections, for the ultimate reality that stands behind music is not only fascinating, but unutterably beautiful.

Bach's young contemporary, Jonathan Edwards, was an ardent lover of music. One of his favorite words was *harmony*. Declaring that the Father, Son and Spirit constitute "the supreme harmony of all," he believed, like Bach, that when we sing together in harmony (as he often did with his family) we do something that reflects God's own beauty.

> The best, most beautiful, and most perfect way that we have of expressing a sweet concord of mind to each other, is by music. When I would form in my mind an idea of a society in the highest degree happy, I think of them as expressing their love, their joy, and the inward concord and harmony and spiritual beauty of their souls by sweetly singing to each other.[11]

There is the deepest and most alluring beauty to be found in the

---

[11]Edwards, "The Miscellanies," in *Works*, 13:329, 331.

heavenly harmony of the Trinity. Karl Barth said: "The triunity of God is the secret of His beauty."[12] Of course. In the lively harmony of the three persons, the radiant love, the overflowing goodness of this God, there is a beauty entirely at odds with the self-serving monotony of single-person gods such as Screwtape described. And because this God has poured out his love and life, we can also say: "The triunity of God is the source of *all* beauty."

1 + 1 = ?

Because we live in a world created by a triune God, it makes sense that different notes can sound together pleasantly, that different colors can complement each other, that things can cohere. In fact, one of the great ironies lies just here: the Trinity is always being pooh-poohed for its supposed mathematical absurdity (1 + 1 + 1 = 1), and yet it is the Trinity that provides the most compelling rationale for mathematics.

At first glance, one might think that math is a discipline which sits a very long way away from any form of religious opinion. Surely 1 + 1 = 2 whether you love Jesus, serve Allah or hug trees. But not so. For monists like Zen Buddhists and Vedantic Hindus, the reality is that everything is one. So I know I appear to be a different person from you, but unfortunately that appearance is a mere illusion to be seen through. I am you. Sorry. For there is no such thing as "2." Ultimately, 1 + 1 = 1.

There needs to be such a thing as ultimate plurality for math to make any real sense, for me to believe that "2" actually means something. And yet there also needs to be such a thing as ultimate unity so that 1 + 1 *always* = 2 and not sometimes 83. To be coherent and meaningful, math requires the existence of ultimate plurality in unity.

What Do the Heavens Declare?
Psalm 19 begins: "The heavens declare the glory of God." It is easy

---

[12]Barth, *Church Dogmatics* II/1, p. 661.

to read that as nothing but a reference to divine power and immensity. You look up at the sky and contemplate the transcendent might and supremacy of the Creator. But God's power tells us only *how* he was able to bring everything into being. It does not tell us *why*.

Now look up to the sky again. The triune God has not merely put a star here and star there; he has lavished the skies with millions and billions of them. As Psalm 19 goes on to say, there in the sky he has placed the sun, which gives warmth, light and life to the world. There too are the clouds which drop down rain to make things grow. The heavens declare the loving generosity of God. And that is why he created.

So next time you look up at the sun, moon and stars and wonder, remember: they are there because God loves, because the Father's love for the Son burst out that it might be enjoyed by many. And they remain there only because God does not stop loving. He is an attentive Father who numbers every hair on our heads, for whom the fall of every sparrow matters; and out of love he upholds all things through his Son, and breathes out natural life on all through his Spirit.

And not only is God's joyful, abundant, spreading goodness the very reason for creation; the love and goodness of the triune God is the source of all love and goodness. The seventeenth-century Puritan theologian John Owen wrote that the Father's love for the Son is "the fountain and prototype of all love. . . . And all love in the creation was introduced from this fountain, to give a shadow and resemblance of it."[13] Indeed, in the triune God is the love behind all love, the life behind all life, the music behind all music, the beauty behind all beauty and the joy behind all joy. In other words, in the triune God is a God we can heartily enjoy—and enjoy in and through his creation.

---

[13]John Owen, "Christologia," in *The Works of John Owen*, ed. William H. Goold, 24 vols. (1850-1855; republished, Edinburgh: Banner of Truth, 1965-1991), 1:144.

Salvation

THE SON SHARES WHAT IS HIS

Twisted Love

The triune God had created a good universe, a place of beauty, joy, harmony and love. It is still a good universe, and we still get to enjoy those things today, but now the harmony is marred by hatred, the joy by pain, the beauty by death. What went wrong? Or, to put it another way, what exactly happened when Adam and Eve sinned in Genesis 3 to make us need salvation?

The answer to that question really depends on what was originally "right." And what "right" looks like depends on what sort of God you have. Take, for instance, the single-person God: this God did not create out of overflowing love, he created merely to rule and be served. In which case, "right" means nothing more than right behavior. Assuming this God, what then went wrong? Quite simply, Adam and Eve did what God had told them not to do. They failed to obey. Now at one level, that is exactly what we see in Genesis 3: the Lord God commanded Adam not to eat from the tree of the knowledge of good and evil, but Adam and Eve did just that.

But that answer does not actually plumb down anywhere near far enough. For in the Bible, sin is something that goes deeper than our behavior. Indeed, we can do what is "right" and be no better than whitewashed tombs, clean on the outside but rotten on the inside. Jonathan Edwards argued that even the demons can do what is "right" in that superficial sense of good behavior:

> The devil once seemed to be religious from fear of torment. Luke 8:28, "When he saw Jesus, he cried out, and fell down before him, and with a loud voice said, What have I to do with thee, Jesus, thou Son of God most high? I beseech thee, torment me not." Here is external worship. The devil is religious; he prays: he prays in a humble posture; he falls down before Christ, he lies prostrate; he prays earnestly, he cries with a loud voice; he uses humble expressions—"I beseech thee, torment me not"—he uses respectful, honorable, adoring expressions—"Jesus, thou Son of God most high." Nothing was wanting but love.[1]

Therein lies the trouble with the story of the single-person God: if sin is simply about *acting* and *behaving* aright, then the devil here is not sinning.

Eve and Adam

What if we start instead with the triune God? How would that change what was "right" in Genesis 2? How would that change what went wrong in Genesis 3? Well, in Genesis 1:27, "God created man in his own image, in the image of God he created him; male and female he created them." That we are made in the image of God could and does mean many things; but the fact

---

[1]Jonathan Edwards, "Writings on the Trinity, Grace, and Faith," in *The Works of Jonathan Edwards,* ed. Sang Hyun Lee (New Haven and London: Yale University Press, 1957–2008), 21:171.

that the God in whose image we are made is specifically the triune God of love has repercussions that echo all through Scripture. Made in the image of this God, we are created to delight in harmonious relationship, to love God, to love each other. Thus Jesus taught that the first and greatest commandment in the law is to love the Lord your God with all your heart and with all your soul and with all your mind, and the second is to love your neighbor as yourself (Mt 22:36-39). That is what we are created for.

What, then, went wrong? It was not that Adam and Eve stopped loving. They were created *as lovers* in the image of God, and they could not undo that. Instead, their love *turned*. When the apostle Paul writes of sinners, he describes them as "lovers of themselves, lovers of money, . . . lovers of pleasure rather than lovers of God" (2 Tim 3:2-4). Lovers we remain, but twisted, our love misdirected and perverted. Created to love God, we turn to love ourselves and anything but God. And this is just what we see in the original sin of Adam and Eve. Eve takes and eats the forbidden fruit because a love for herself—and gaining wisdom for herself—has overcome any love she might have had for God.

"When the woman saw that the fruit of the tree was good for food and *pleasing* to the eye, *and also desirable* for gaining wisdom, she took some and ate it" (Gen 3:6). The problem is deeper than her actions, deeper than outward disobedience. Her *act* of sin was merely the manifestation of the turn in her heart: she now desired the fruit more than she desired God. And this, says James, is just how it is with all sin: it flows from our desires, from what we wrongly love: "Each one is tempted when, by his own evil desire, he is dragged away and enticed. Then, after desire has conceived, it gives birth to sin; and sin, when it is full-grown, gives birth to death" (Jas 1:14-15).

Similar themes crop up in Ezekiel's lament concerning the king of Tyre. There, the Lord addresses the king, saying: "You were in Eden, the garden of God; every precious stone adorned you: ruby, topaz and emerald, chrysolite, onyx and jasper, sapphire, turquoise and beryl. Your settings and mountings were made of gold; on the day you were created they were prepared. You were anointed as *a guardian cherub*, for so I ordained you" (Ezek 28:13-14). All these precious stones set in gold that he wears are surely reminding us of Israel's high priest, who would wear twelve gemstones on a golden breastpiece as he served before the ark of the covenant in the tabernacle. And there on the ark of the covenant were two golden *cherubs*, their eyes fixed on the mercy seat (the lid of the ark), where the Lord was supposed to sit, enthroned (Lev 16:2; 1 Sam 4:4).

Then something goes wrong in Ezekiel. The Lord says to this cherub: "Your heart became proud on account of your beauty, and you corrupted your wisdom because of your splendor" (Ezek 28:17). In other words, just as Eve's desires turned in on herself, so the cherub's gaze turned in on himself. That is what went wrong in Eden, the garden of God: those who were made to enjoy the beauty of the Lord turned away to enjoy their own. Love's longings and the desires of their hearts shifted from the Lord to themselves. And thus, instead of running to him, they would now hide from him.

John Milton sought to capture this in *Paradise Lost* by writing of Eve's ominous infatuation with her own reflection. Before she actually took the forbidden fruit, we are told, her gaze had already began to focus on herself. It begins beside a clear smooth lake, and Eve bends down to look:

As I bent down to look, just opposite
A shape within the watery gleam appeared,
Bending to look on me: I started back,
It started back; but pleased I soon returned,
Pleased it returned as soon with answering looks
Of sympathy and love: There I had fixed
Mine eyes till now, and pined with vain desire.[2]

[2]John Milton, *Paradise Lost*, IV, II, pp. 460-66.

TWO DIFFERENT GOSPELS

Everyone likes preachers who give challenging sermons, and none have ever been more challenging than Pelagius. Somewhere around the turn of the fifth century, he arrived in Rome, lambasting immorality and issuing a clarion call for Christians to live in purity. All stirring stuff.

However, when Augustine, the planet-brained bishop of Hippo, looked into what Pelagius was teaching, he realized that, for all his Christian language, Pelagius had fundamentally misunderstood the nature of God and the gospel. Pelagius was teaching that we had done wrong things—that was the problem—but that if ever we are to enter heaven, we must start doing right things. It did not seem to have occurred to Pelagius that we were created to

Augustine reading St. Paul

know and *love* God, and thus for him the aim of the Christian life was not to enjoy God but to *use* him as the one who sells us heaven for the price of being moral.

How differently Augustine saw things! Knowing God to be the triune God of love, he held that we were not created simply to live under his moral code, hoping for some paradise where he will never be. We were made to find our rest and satisfaction in his all-satisfying fellowship. Moreover, our problem is not so much that we have behaved wrongly, but that we have been drawn to love wrongly. Made in the image of the God of love, Augustine argued that we are *always* motivated by love—and that is why Adam and Eve disobeyed God. They sinned because they loved something else more than him. That also means that merely altering our behavior, as Pelagius suggested, will do no good. Something much more profound is needed: our hearts must be turned back.

A little over a thousand years later, Martin Luther picked up Augustine's line of thought to define the sinner as "the person curved in on himself," no longer outgoingly loving like God, no longer looking to God, but inward-looking, self-obsessed, devilish. Such a person might well behave morally or religiously, but all they did would simply express their fundamental love for themselves.

As God the Father has always looked outward to the Son and vice versa, so Eve was created to look outward, to look like God and to enjoy God as the source of all goodness and life. But Eve was turning inward to love only herself. And thus she was turning from the image of God into the image of the devil.

The nature of the triune God makes all the difference in the world to understanding what went wrong when Adam and Eve fell. It means something happened deeper than rule-breaking and misbehavior: we perverted love and rejected *him,* the one who made us to love and be loved by him.

God So Loved . . .

Astonishingly, it was this very rejection of God that then drew forth the extreme depths of his love. In his response to sin we see deeper than ever into the very being of God. "Whoever does not love does not know God, because *God is love. This is how God showed his love among us: He sent his one and only Son into the world* that we might live through him. This is love: not that we loved God, but that he loved us and sent his Son as an atoning sacrifice for our sins" (1 Jn 4:8-10).

The God who is love definitively displays that love to the world by sending us his eternally beloved Son to atone for our sin. And so, through the sending of the Son for our salvation we see more clearly than ever how generous and self-giving the love of the triune God is.

Without the cross, we could never have imagined the depth and seriousness of what it means to say that God is love. "*This* is how we know what love is: Jesus Christ laid down his life for us" (1 Jn 3:16). On the cross we see the great holiness of God's love, that the light of his pure love will destroy the darkness of sin and evil. On the cross we see the intensity and strength of his love, that it is not an insipid thing at all, but majestically strong as it faces death, battles evil and gives life. For Christ was not bound against his will and dragged to a crucifixion he did not choose. Nobody could take his life from him, he said. "I lay it down of my own accord. I have authority to lay it down and authority to take it up again. This command I received from my Father" (Jn 10:18). Jesus' self-giving love is entirely unconstrained and free. It comes, not from any necessity, but entirely out of who he is, the glory of his Father. Through the cross we see a God who delights to give himself.

But *why* did the Father send his Son to us? A good enough reason seems to be given in John 3:16, "*God so loved the world* that he gave his one and only Son." That is stunning enough, but later on in John's Gospel, Jesus speaks of an even more primal and potent reason. Praying to his Father, Jesus says: "Righteous Father, though the world does not know you, I know you, and they know that you have sent me. I have made you known to them, and will continue to make you known in order that the love you have for me may be in them and that I myself may be in them" (Jn 17:25-26).

That is, the Father sent his Son to make himself known— meaning not that he wanted simply to download some information about himself, but *that the love the Father eternally had for the Son might be in those who believe in him, and that we might enjoy the Son as the Father always has.* Here, then, is a salvation no single-person God could offer even if they wanted to: the Father so delights in his eternal love for the Son that he desires to share it with all who will believe. Ultimately, the Father sent the Son because the Father so loved the Son—and wanted to share that love and fellowship. His love for the world is the overflow of his almighty love for his Son.

In fact, just a few verses earlier, Jesus puts it even more provocatively, saying to his Father, "I have given them [those who believe] the glory that you gave me" (Jn 17:22). Those are words to cause a heart attack, because in Isaiah 42:8 the Lord clearly and emphatically states: "I am the LORD; that is my name! I *will not* give my glory to another." How then can Jesus possibly give his glory?

Yet the Lord God in Isaiah 42 is not a single-person God, desperately hugging himself and refusing to share as he whines: "I will not give my glory to another." In Isaiah 42, the Lord is speaking of his servant, his chosen one, the one he anoints with his Spirit (Is 42:1). That is, the Father is speaking of his anointed Son, the one who will not break a bruised reed or snuff out a smoldering wick (Is 42:3; see Mt 12:15-21, where Jesus is said to fulfill Isaiah's prophecy). In fact, the Lord turns to address him directly:

> I, the LORD, have called you in righteousness; I will take hold of your hand. I will keep you and will make you to be a covenant for the people and a light for the Gentiles, to open eyes that are blind, to free captives from prison and to release from the dungeon those who sit in darkness. I am the LORD; that is my name! I will not give my glory to another. (Is 42:6-8)

In other words, far from hoarding his glory, the Father gives it, freely and fully, to his Son. It is simply that he will give it to *no other* than his Son.

Now left at that, this could still look like a limited, restrained generosity. It is certainly better than a single-person God's complete refusal to share, but the exclusivity of it doesn't immediately strike one as great good news to rejoice in. In fact, though, this is at the heart of why the triune God's salvation is so infinitely superior to the salvation offered by any other god. For the Father gives *all* his glory, his love, his blessing, his very self exclusively to his Son—and he then sends his Son to share with us his fullness. "I have given them the glory that you gave me."

The Father, then, is not about sprinkling blessings from afar, and his salvation is not about being kept at a distance, merely pitied and forgiven by our Creator. Instead, he pours all his blessing out on his Son, and then sends him that we might share his glorious fullness. The Father so loves that he desires to catch us up into that loving fellowship he enjoys with the Son. And that means I can know God as he truly is: as Father. In fact, I can know the Father as *my* Father.

Now how? How possibly can my Creator come to treat me as he treats his Son?

Our Great High Priest

John 17 pulls the curtain back especially wide. It is a passage traditionally known as Jesus' "high priestly prayer," and that because it alludes to the work of the Old Testament high priests of Israel—men like Moses' brother Aaron—who were appointed to come before the Lord *on behalf of God's people,* and particularly to bring the blood of the annual sacrifice of atonement into the Lord's presence.

The first thing about Israel's high priests was that they had to be Israelites (of the tribe of Levi), sharing the very flesh and blood of God's people. So, in becoming the true and ultimate high priest, God the Son came from heaven and took our flesh and blood, becoming one of us.

> Since the children have flesh and blood, he too shared in
> their humanity so that by his death he might destroy him
> who holds the power of death—that is, the devil—and free

those who all their lives were held in slavery by their fear of death. For surely it is not angels he helps, but Abraham's descendants. For this reason he had to be made like his brothers in every way, in order that he might become a merciful and faithful high priest in service to God, and that he might make atonement for the sins of the people. (Heb 2:14-17)

The high priest with a burnt offering on the Day of Atonement

The big red-letter event in each high priest's diary was Yom Kippur, the Day of Atonement (Lev 16). On that day, he would symbolically sacrifice a goat which would die for the sins of the people, and he would bring its blood into the very presence of the Lord in the tabernacle. It was all just symbolic, of course, "because it is impossible for the blood of bulls and goats to take away sins. Therefore, when Christ came into the world, he said: 'Sacrifice and offering you did not desire, but a body you prepared for me'" (Heb 10:4-5).

On the true Day of Atonement, Christ the High Priest would sacrifice not a goat, but his own body—our flesh and blood—on the cross.

That moment of self-sacrifice would come in John 19, but in John 17 Jesus shows what it would all accomplish. For in John 17 Jesus goes about the more ordinary work of the high priest—*work that depended on that sacrificial act of atonement*. And what was

WHEN I SAW THE CROSS, I SAW THE TRINITY

The wonder is that it is *the Son* who hangs on the cross. The Father, in his great love, sends the Son; and the Son, delighting to do the will of the Father, and sharing his Father's love, goes. Indeed, that love and delight make the Son unstoppable: he resolutely sets his face to go to Jerusalem where he will die; he rebukes Peter for even suggesting otherwise; he trembles at the thought of it, but lays his life down entirely of his own accord (Jn 10:18). For he, the Son, desires to be both the high priest and the sacrifice for sin, offering himself up to his Father through the Spirit (Heb 9:14).

It means that this God makes no third party suffer to achieve atonement. The one who dies is the lamb of God, the Son. And it means that nobody but God contributes to the work of salvation: the Father, Son and Spirit accomplish it all. Now if God were not triune, if there was no Son, no lamb of God to die in our place, then we would have to atone for our sin ourselves. We would have to provide, for God could not. But—hallelujah!—God has a Son, and in his infinite kindness he dies, paying the wages of sin, *for us*. It is *because* God is triune that the cross is such good news.

that work? Every day, the high priest was to offer a sweet-smelling incense before the Lord in the tabernacle (Ex 30:7-10), and he was to do so while wearing over his heart a golden plate onto which were fixed twelve jewels. Each of those jewels was inscribed with the name of one of the tribes of Israel (Ex 28:15-29). Thus the high priest would be in the presence of the Lord with the people of God, as it were, on his heart.

All that is precisely what Jesus is about in John 17: he comes before God his Father with the incense of his prayers (as a pleasing smell rising before the Lord, incense is symbolic of prayer, Psalm 141:2; Revelation 5:8). And he does so with the people of God on his heart: "My prayer is not for them [the apostles] alone. I pray also for those who will believe in me through their message" (Jn 17:20). In other words, as Israel's high priest would symbolically bring the people of God before the Lord by that plate over his heart, so Christ would bring us, in him, before his Father. God the Son came from his Father, became one of us, died our death—and all to bring us back with him to be before his Father like the jewels on the heart of the high priest.

Jesus' first prayer for all his people is "that all of them may be one, Father, . . . that they may be one as we are one: I in them and you in me. *May they be brought to complete unity*" (Jn 17:21-23). It is a highly appropriate prayer for Jesus to pray as our high priest, for Psalm 133 begins: "How good and pleasant it is when brothers live together in unity! It is like precious oil poured on the head, running down on the beard, running down on Aaron's beard, down upon the collar of his robes" (Ps 133:1-2).

The psalm is referring to the ordination of Aaron as high priest, where the sacred anointing oil would be poured out on his head (Lev 8:12). Just so would Christ ("the Anointed One") be anointed

Ordination of Aaron

by the Spirit at his baptism. And as the oil ran down from Aaron's head to his body, so the Spirit would run down from Christ our Head to his Body, the church. Thus *we* become "partakers of his anointing."[3] The Spirit, through whom the Father had

---

[3]Heidelberg Catechism, 32.

eternally loved his Son, would now anoint believers "that they may be one as we are one" (Jn 17:22). One with the Lord, one with each other.

This is salvation with jam on top. In fact, the more trinitarian the salvation, the sweeter it is. For it is not just that we are brought before the Father in the Son; we receive the Spirit with which he was anointed. Jesus said in John 16:14 that the Spirit "will bring glory to me by taking from what is mine and making it known to you." The Spirit takes what is the Son's and makes it ours. When the Spirit rested upon the Son at his baptism, Jesus heard the Father declare from heaven: "You are my Son, whom I love; with you I am well pleased." But now that the same Spirit of sonship rests on me, the same words apply to me: in Christ my high priest I am an adopted, beloved, Spirit-anointed son. As Jesus says to the Father in John 17:23, you "have loved them even as you have loved me." And so, as the Son brings me before his Father, with their Spirit in me *I* can boldly cry, "Abba," for their fellowship I now freely share: the Most High *my* Father, the Son my great brother, the Spirit no longer Jesus' Comforter alone, but mine.

As Loved as the Son

John 1:18 describes God the Son as being eternally in the bosom or lap of the Father. One would never dare imagine it, but Jesus declares that his desire is that believers might be with him there (Jn 17:24). That, indeed, is why the Father sent him, that we who have rejected him might be brought back—and brought back, not merely as creatures, but as children, to enjoy the abounding love the Son has always known.

J. I. Packer once wrote: "If you want to judge how well a person understands Christianity, find out how much he makes of the thought of being God's child, and having God as his Father. If this is not the thought that prompts and controls his worship and prayers and his whole outlook on life, it means he does not understand Christianity very well at all."[4]

Indeed, for when a person deliberately and confidently calls the Almighty "Father," it shows they have grasped something beautiful and fundamental about who God is and to what they have been saved. And how that wins our hearts back to him! For the fact that God the Father is happy and even delights to share his love for his Son and thus be known as *our* Father reveals just how unfathomably gracious and kind he is.

And it really is with ungrudging delight that he gives us that privilege. When someone comes to faith, Christians often smile and say (with an allusion to Luke 15:10) that the angels will be rejoicing in heaven. But what Luke 15:10 actually says is that there is joy in heaven *before* the angels of God over one sinner who repents. Who is before the angels of God in heaven? God. It is God, first and foremost, who rejoices to lavish his love on those who have rejected him.

Knowing God as our Father not only wonderfully gladdens our view of him; it gives the deepest comfort and joy. The honor of it is stupefying. To be the child of some rich king would be nice; but to be the beloved of the emperor of the universe is beyond words. Clearly the salvation of this God is better even than forgiveness, and certainly more secure. Other gods might offer forgiveness, but this God welcomes and embraces us as his children, never to send us away. (For children do not get disowned for being naughty.) He does not offer some kind of "he loves me, he loves me not" relationship whereby I have to try and keep myself in his favor by behaving impeccably. No, "to all who received him, to those who believed in his name, he gave the right to become children of God" (Jn 1:12)—and so with security to enjoy his love forever.

Think of just who the Son is: he is the one eternally and utterly loved by his Father; the Father would not ever moderate or re-

---

[4]J. I. Packer, *Knowing God* (London: Hodder & Stoughton, 1973), p. 224.

nounce his love for his Son—and the Son comes to share *that,* as the Father wanted. Because Jesus is not ashamed to call us brothers (Heb 2:11), his Father is not ashamed to be known as ours (Heb 11:16). Nothing could give greater confidence and delight in approaching the heavenly throne of grace. "How great is the love the Father has lavished on us, that we should be called children of God! And that is what we are!" (1 Jn 3:1).

The Difference Between a Father and a Führer

Now imagine a God who is not Father, Son and Spirit: never in its wildest dreams could it muster up such a salvation. If God was not a Father, he could never give us the right to be his children. If he did not enjoy eternal fellowship with his Son, one has to wonder if he would have any fellowship to share with us, or if he would even know what fellowship looks like. If, for example, the Son was a creature and had not eternally been "in the bosom of the Father," knowing him and being loved by him, what sort of relationship with the Father could he share with us? If the Son himself had never been close to the Father, how could he bring us close?

If God was a single person, salvation would look entirely different. He might allow us to live under his rule and protection, but at an infinite distance, approached, perhaps, through intermediaries. He might even offer forgiveness, but he would not offer closeness. And, since by definition he would not be eternally loving, would he deal with the price of sin himself and offer that forgiveness for free? Most unlikely. Distant hirelings we would remain, never to hear the Son's golden words to his Father: "You have loved them even as you have loved me."

But this God comes to us himself, the Father rejoicing to share his love for his Son, sending him that in him we might be brought back into the Father's bosom, there by the Spirit to call him "Abba."

HATING GOD AND LOVING THE FATHER

The Reformer Martin Luther knew well how much the Fatherhood of God changes the shape of salvation and all our thoughts about God. As a monk, his mind was filled with the knowledge that God is righteous and hates sin, but he failed to see any further into who God is—what his righteousness is and *why* he hates sin.

ÆTHERNA IPSE SVAE MENTIS SIMVLACHRA LVTHERVS
EXPRIMIT AT VVLTVS CERA LVCAE OCCIDVOS.
· M · D · X X ·

The monk Martin Luther (1483-1546)

The result, he said, was that "I did not love, yes, I hated the righteous God who punishes sinners, and secretly, if not blasphemously, certainly murmuring greatly, I was angry with God."[a] Not knowing God as a kind and willing Father, a God who brings us close, Luther found he could not love him. He and his fellow monks transferred their affections to Mary and various other saints; it was them they would love and to them they would pray.

That changed when he began to see that God is a fatherly God who shares, who gives to us his righteousness, glory and wisdom. Looking back later in life he reflected that, as a monk, he had not actually been worshiping the right God, for it is "not enough," he then said, to know God as the Creator and Judge. Only when God is known as a loving Father is he known aright. "For although the whole world has most carefully sought to understand the nature, mind and activity of God, it has had no success in this whatever. But . . . God Himself has revealed and disclosed the deepest profundity of his fatherly heart, His sheer inexpressible love."[b]

Through sending his Son to bring us back to himself, God has revealed himself to be inexpressibly loving and supremely fatherly. What Luther found was that not only does that give great assurance and joy— it also wins our hearts to him, for "we may look into His fatherly heart and sense how boundlessly He loves us. That would warm our hearts, setting them aglow with thankfulness."[c] In the salvation of this God we see a God we can really love.

[a]Martin Luther, "Preface to the Complete Edition of Luther's Latin Writings," in *Luther's Works*, ed. J. Pelikan (vols. 1-30, St. Louis: Concordia; vols. 31-55, Philadelphia: Fortress, 1955-1976), 34:336-37.
[b]Martin Luther, *Luther's Large Catechism* (St. Louis: Concordia, 1978), p. 77.
[c]Ibid., p. 70.

The Son Shares His Knowledge of the Father

"For although the whole world has most carefully sought to understand the nature, mind and activity of God, it has had no success in this whatever," wrote Luther. His fellow Reformer, John Calvin, put it even more bluntly (and to be blunter than Luther is always impressive):

The greatest geniuses are blinder than moles! . . . They never even sensed that assurance of God's benevolence toward us (without which man's understanding can only be filled with boundless confusion). Human reason, therefore, neither approaches, nor strives toward, nor even takes a straight aim at, this truth: to understand who the true God is or what sort of God he wishes to be toward us.[5]

Luther and Calvin had in mind verses like Matthew 11:27, "No one knows the Son except the Father, and no one knows the Father except the Son and those to whom the Son chooses to reveal him," and John 1:18, "No one has ever seen God, but God the One and Only, who is at the Father's side, has made him

[5]John Calvin, *Institutes of the Christian Religion* 2.2.18.

known." In short, if God had no word to say to us, we simply would not know him or dream of his deep benevolence.

Of course, if God is a single person, and has always been alone, why should he speak? In the loneliness of eternity before creation, who would he have spoken to? And why would he start now? The habit of keeping himself to himself would run deep. Such a God would be far more likely to remain unknown.

But what if somehow such a God did have a word to say? Here we are not left to guesswork: the Qur'an is a perfect example of a solitary God's word. Allah is a single-person God who has an eternal word beside him in heaven, the Qur'an. At a glance, that seems to make Allah look less eternally lonely. But what is so significant is the fact that Allah's word is a *book,* not a true companion for him. And it is a book that is only *about* him. Thus when Allah gives us his Qur'an, he gives us some *thing,* a deposit of information about himself and how he likes things.

However, when the triune God gives us his Word, he gives us his very self, for the Son is the Word of God, the perfect revelation of his Father. The Word was with God and the Word *was* God. It is all, well, very revealing. This God does not give us some *thing* that is other than himself, or merely tell us *about* himself; he actually gives us himself. If he just dropped a book from heaven, he could keep us at the sort of distance we would expect. But he doesn't. The very Word of God who is God comes to us and dwells with us.

And so, in Jesus Christ the Word of God we see the most revealing revelation. In Jesus we see that God is Father, Son and Spirit, for he is beloved by the Father and anointed with the Spirit. In Jesus we see a God so generous and kind that he gives himself to us and comes to be with us. And since the Son is "the image of the invisible God" (Col 1:15), "the radiance of God's glory and the exact representation of his being" (Heb 1:3), we may know, as he says, that "anyone who has seen me has seen the Father" (Jn 14:9). If he were not truly God, of the very being of the Father, he could not truly reveal God and we would be left wondering if the God he represented is really as good as he. But given who he is, we may confidently and deliberately say that in Jesus *we know God.* For he is God himself, and he comes, not only to share the love of the Father with us, but also to share his knowledge of the Father with us. He comes that we might grow to know the Father as he knows the Father. Wonderfully, then, because God is Father, Son and Spirit—because the Father has a Word who is God, of his very being, and who is with him and who knows him—we can know him, and know him with an intimacy no other God could allow.

Then there is the Spirit—and more and more this chapter is straining to get onto the next one, for there is so much to say about the Spirit. For now, though, let us note just one thing: in revealing himself, not only does the Father send his Son in the power of his Spirit; together the Father and the Son send the Spirit to make the Son known. The Son makes the Father known; the Spirit makes the Son known.

From the top right, a scroll is unwound so that Matthew the Evangelist receives words from heaven into his inkhorn, inspiration for his Gospel.

He does this first of all by breathing out the Scriptures (2 Tim 3:16; 1 Pet 1:11-12) so that in them, the "word of Christ," Christ may be known (Rom 10:17; Col 3:16).

Does this mean that we are, in fact, back to God just giving us a book, as in Islam? Far from it, for—as we shall see if you can bear the wait—God the Spirit not only inspires Scripture, he also comes to us. Indeed, he comes *into* us. There could be no greater intimacy than with this God.

What it does mean is that the point of all the Scriptures is to make Christ known. As the Son makes his Father known, so the Spirit-breathed Scriptures make the Son known. Paul wrote to Timothy of how "from infancy you have known the holy Scriptures, which are able to make you wise for salvation through faith in Christ Jesus" (2 Tim 3:15). He is referring to the Old Testament, of course, but the same could be said of the New. Similarly, Jesus said to the Jews of his day: "You diligently study the Scriptures because you think that by them you possess eternal life. These are the Scriptures that testify about me, yet you refuse to come to me to have life. . . . If you believed Moses, you would believe me, for he wrote about me" (Jn 5:39-40, 46).

Clearly, Jesus believed that it is quite possible to study the Scriptures diligently and entirely miss their point, which is to proclaim him so that readers might come to him for life.

Who Is It You Are Looking For?

It all dramatically affects why we open the Bible. We can open our Bibles for all sorts of odd reasons—as a religious duty, an attempt to earn God's favor, or thinking that it serves as a moral self-help guide, a manual of handy tips for effective religious lives. That idea is actually one main reason so many feel discouraged in their Bible-reading. Hoping to find quick lessons for how they should spend today, people find instead a genealogy, or a list of various sacrifices. And how could page after page of histories, descriptions of the temple, instructions to priests, affect how I rest, work and pray today?

But when you see that Christ is the subject of all the Scriptures, that he is the Word, the Lord, the Son who reveals his Father, the promised Hope, the true Temple, the true Sacrifice, the great High Priest, the ultimate King, then you can read, not so much asking, "What does this mean for me, right now?" but "What do I learn here of Christ?" Knowing that the Bible is about him and not me means that, instead of reading the Bible obsessing about me, I can gaze on him. And as through the pages you get caught up in the wonder of his story, you find your heart strangely pounding for him in a way you never would have if you had treated the Bible as a book about you.

Or let me speak as a preacher. Just occasionally, when I am invited to preach somewhere, things go like this:

READER: *(reads set Bible passage very nicely and then says)* This is the word of the Lord.

PEOPLE: *(mumble)*

LEADER: Thank you, Reader. And now, I'm afraid, Reeves is going to come and try to explain that passage to us.

REEVES: *(thinks to himself)* Oh no, I'm not! This isn't going to be some English Comprehension exercise. I intend to proclaim the word of God! *(walks to pulpit/lectern, trying to shake off grumpiness)*

I know, it's a bit pedantic, but it comes from the fear that we'll merely study the Scriptures as interesting texts instead of hearing them as God's very words that hold out Christ and draw us to *want* him. For the Spirit breathed out those words, not that we might merely alter our behavior, not that we might merely know *about* Christ, but that, as John Calvin wrote, we might have a "sincere affection" for him, that we might "cordially embrace him."[6] Charles Spurgeon, the twinkle-eyed master-preacher of the nine-

---

[6]John Calvin, *Commentary on John* (Edinburgh: Calvin Translation Society, 1844-1856; repr., Grand Rapids: Baker, 1993), 16.27.

teenth century, put it like this: "The motto of all true servants of
God must be, 'We preach Christ, and him crucified.' A sermon
without Christ in it is like a loaf of bread without any flour in it.
No Christ in your sermon, sir? Then go home, and never preach
again until you have something worth preaching."[7]

Yes! For Christ is the Word of God. Without him we would be
"blinder than moles," never dreaming of how fatherly God is. But
the Spirit-breathed Scriptures proclaim him as the radiance of his
Father, the only one who can share with us the true life of knowing,
loving and being loved by his Father.

---

[7]Charles Spurgeon, "Sermon 2899," in *Metropolitan Tabernacle Pulpit: Sermons* (London: Passmore & Alabaster, 1904), 50:431.

The Christian Life

THE SPIRIT BEAUTIFIES

The Spirit of Life

The first thing the Nicene Creed says about the Spirit is that he is "the Lord, the giver of life." In the beginning, it was the Spirit who, like a mother dove, first vitalized creation and breathed life into it; likewise it is the Spirit who gives *new* life—first to Jesus in the tomb (Rom 8:11), and then to us.

Now just to have said that is to have said something profound: that we do not have life in ourselves. We depend entirely on the Spirit. And if that is how we were created to be, how much more is that true of us now! For when Adam and Eve turned away from God in Genesis 3, they turned to death. As a result, we all come into the world spiritually stillborn, dead in our transgressions and sins (Eph 2:1). "Death" here, of course, doesn't mean nonexistence; rather, it is that, like Adam and Eve, our hearts are turned from the Lord. Naturally we love and desire other things—ourselves especially—and not him who is the source of life.

That is a real problem, for we are made to follow our hearts, to do what we want. As Adam and Eve followed their hearts' desires when they first sinned, so we continue. "In his heart a man plans his course" (Prov 16:9). But if we do not want—if our hearts do not desire—the Lord of life, then we will never choose him, and so we must remain prisoners of death. There is no hope of life to

A LUST FOR LIFE

A man who knew all this very personally was William Tyndale, the linguistic genius who first translated the bulk of the Bible from its

original Hebrew and Greek into English. He grew up believing that Christianity was largely a matter of externals—of right behavior and right ritual. Through his avid reading of Scripture, though, he came to see that his thinking had been topsy-turvy at best.

As he would write later, sin is not "that outward work only committed by the body"; rather, all sinful acts spring from "the heart,

William Tyndale (1494?-1536)

be found within ourselves. Martin Luther thus wrote that the first thing belief in the Spirit means is that "by my own reason or strength I cannot believe in Jesus Christ, my Lord, or come to him. But the Holy Spirit has called me through the Gospel."[1]

Since our problem is with our hearts, the Spirit gives us new birth into a new life precisely by giving us new hearts (Ezek 36:26; Jn 3:3-8). The tool he uses is Scripture (1 Pet 1:23; Jas 1:18), but through Scripture he opens our blinded eyes to see who the Lord truly and beautifully is and so he wins our hearts back to him. And *that* is life—to know him (Jn 17:3).

[1]Martin Luther, "The Small Catechism," in *The Book of Concord: The Confessions of the Evangelical Lutheran Church*, trans. and ed. Theodore G. Tappert (Philadelphia: Fortress, 1959), p. 345.

with all the powers, affections, and appetites, wherewith we can but sin. . . . The scripture looketh singularly unto the heart, and unto the root and original fountain of all sin; which is unbelief in the bottom of the heart." Our problem is with our desires, that naturally we have no appetite for God, and we place all our affections elsewhere. Our only hope of life is to be found with the Spirit, who "bringeth lust [that is, desire!], looseth the heart, maketh him free, setteth him at liberty."[a]

Such phrases crop up a lot in Tyndale's writings and, like furrows of white on the surface of the sea, they show that something powerful is moving beneath. For if the Spirit's first work in salvation is to loose our hearts that we might have a lust or desire for the Lord, then the Christian life is about so much more than "getting heaven." The Spirit is about drawing us into the divine life. The Father has eternally delighted in the Son through the Spirit, and the Son in the Father; the Spirit's work in giving us new life, then, is nothing less than bringing us to share in their mutual delight.

[a]William Tyndale, "A Prologue upon the Epistle of St. Paul to the Romans," in *The Works of William Tyndale* (Edinburgh and Carlisle, Penn.: Banner of Truth, 2010), 1:489.

The Spirit Gives Himself

The life that the Spirit gives is not some abstract thing. In fact, it is not primarily some *thing* that he gives at all. The Spirit gives us his very self, that we might know and enjoy him and so enjoy his fellowship with the Father and the Son. The Puritan theologian Thomas Goodwin wrote that "not only God doth bless with all other good things, but above all by communicating *himself* and his own blessedness." We saw earlier that many theologians have liked to compare God to a fountain, in that his very being is about pouring forth life and love. Another image theologians have liked to use of God is that of the radiant sun (following verses like Psalm 84:11 and John 8:12), and it is to the sun that Goodwin then compares God: "The sun doth not only enrich the earth with all

good things . . . but glads and refreshes all with shedding immediately *its own wings* of light and warmth, which is so pleasant to
behold and enjoy. And thus doth God, and Christ the Sun of
righteousness."[2]

As the sun gives *of itself*—its own light and warmth—in shining
on us, so God gives us himself and the blessedness he has always
enjoyed. He does so in giving us his Son, and he does so in giving
us his Spirit.

This is one of those truths that is a bit like silver—easily tar-
nished and covered with grime. When Christians talk of God
giving us "grace," for example, we can quickly imagine that "grace"
is some kind of spiritual pocket money he doles out. Even the old
explanation that "grace" is "God's Riches At Christ's Expense"
can make it sound like stuff that God gives. But the word *grace* is
really just a shorthand way of speaking about the personal and
loving kindness out of which, ultimately, God gives *himself*.

We are getting close now to the heart of the Reformation in the
sixteenth century. In medieval Roman Catholicism, grace had
come to be seen as "stuff": Catholics would pray "Hail, Mary, *full
of* grace," as if Mary were a bottle and grace like milk. The fallout
from this belief can be felt in the seminal debate in 1539 between
(in the red corner) the Roman Catholic Cardinal Sadoleto and (in
the blue corner) the Reformer John Calvin.

One of Sadoleto's arguments against the message of the Reformation was that, if it is preached that God saves people by his grace
alone, people will be given no reason to want holiness. After all, if
my holiness does not contribute in any way to my getting saved,
why should I bother? I've got "grace," after all. It was a powerful jab
to Calvin's theological head, but the Reformer replied with a
knockout blow: that Sadoleto had fundamentally misunderstood
salvation, as if it were something other than being brought to know,

---

[2]Thomas Goodwin, *The Works of Thomas Goodwin* (Edinburgh: James Nichol, 1861),
1:46, my emphasis.

John Calvin preparing to skewer Cardinal Sadoleto

love and so want to please a beautifully holy God. For Calvin, salvation was not about getting some *thing* called "grace"—it was about freely receiving the Spirit, and so the Father and the Son.

A problem similar to Sadoleto's happens when the Spirit is thought of as a force and not a person. Again it gives the impression of God up in heaven lobbing down tokens of his blessing ("the force") while himself remaining all distant. And if that is how it is, then I can hardly have communion with this force (or with the Father or the Son): the Spirit must be a power I am to get hold of and use as I get on with my life. Some do magic; others have money and the latest beauty products; I use the Spirit. And if I manage to use the Spirit more than other Christians, hurrah for spiritual me.

How different to know that the Spirit is as real a person as Jesus Christ, and that he comes to live in me! R. A. Torrey put it (rather quaintly) like this:

How often some young man has had his hand on the door of some place of sin that he is about to enter and the thought has come to him, "If I should enter there, my mother might hear of it and it would nearly kill her," and he has turned his back on that door and gone away to lead a pure life, that he might not grieve his mother. But there is One who is holier than any mother, One who is more sensitive against sin than the purest woman who ever walked this earth, and who loves us as even no mother ever loved. This One dwells in our hearts, if we are really Christians, and He sees every act we do by day or under cover of the night; He hears every word we utter in public or in private; He sees every thought we entertain, He beholds every fancy and imagination that is permitted even a momentary lodging in our mind, and if there is anything unholy, impure, selfish, mean, petty, unkind, harsh, unjust, or any evil act or word or thought or fancy, He is grieved by it.[3]

It is not just the grief our sin might cause him; the Spirit's personal presence in us means we are brought to enjoy the Spirit's own intimate communion with the Father and the Son. If the Spirit were not God, he could not do that. It is all because God is three persons—Father, Son and Spirit—that we can have such communion. If God was in heaven and his Spirit a mere force, he would be more distant than the moon.

The Oxygen of the New Life

The life the Spirit gives is not an abstract package of blessing; it is his own life that he shares with us, the life of fellowship with the Father and the Son. Thus the Spirit is not like some divine milkman, leaving the gift of "life" on our doorsteps only to move on. In giving us life he comes in to be with us and remain with us. Having once given life, then, he does not move on; he stays to make that life blossom and grow.

---

[3]R. A. Torrey, *The Person and Work of the Holy Spirit* (New York: Fleming H. Revell, 1910), p. 15.

"Where the Spirit is, there it is always summer," wrote William Tyndale, for there "there are always good fruits, that is to say, good works."[4] Tyndale was not just picking any old image at random—the warmth of the Spirit's summer is important, for just as the Spirit first makes us warm with life by turning our hearts and their desires to Christ, so he continues to warm us. The new life the Spirit gives *is* a life of warmth, for it is his own life of delighting in the Father and the Son, and he rears us up precisely by warming our hearts to them.

Jonathan Edwards expanded on Tyndale's image like this:

> All shall stand about the God of glory, the fountain of love, as it were opening their bosoms to be filled with those effusions of love which are poured forth from thence, as the flowers on the earth in a pleasant spring day open their bosoms to the sun to be filled with his warmth and light, and to flourish in beauty and fragrancy by his rays. Every saint is as a flower in the garden of God, and holy love is the fragrancy and sweet odor which they all send forth, and with which they fill that paradise.[5]

Though he does not say as much here, Edwards is describing the work of the Spirit, how "God has poured out his love into our hearts by the Holy Spirit, whom he has given us" (Rom 5:5). It is how the Spirit breathes out his life on us: he enlightens us to know the love of God, and that light warms us, drawing us to love him and to overflow with love to others.

How, though, does the Spirit enlighten us to know the love of God? Quite simply, by opening our eyes to see the glory of Christ. That is how he comforts believers. As Jesus said, "When the Counselor comes, whom I will send to you from the Father, the Spirit of

---

[4]Tyndale, "A Prologue upon the Epistle of St. Paul to the Romans," in *Works,* 1:499.
[5]Jonathan Edwards, "Ethical Writings," in *The Works of Jonathan Edwards,* ed. Paul Ramsey (New Haven and London: Yale University Press, 1957-2008), 8:386.

Moses with one of the tablets of stone

truth who goes out from the Father, *he will testify about me*" (Jn 15:26). Knowing Christ—and through him, the Father— is the life the Spirit gives. In 2 Corinthians 3, Paul writes of how Moses' face came to shine from having been with the Lord, and that likewise it is by beholding the glory of the Lord in the gospel that we ourselves "are being transformed into his likeness with ever-increasing glory, which comes from the Lord, who is the Spirit" (2 Cor 3:18). With 2 Corinthians 3 in mind, Richard Sibbes wrote:

The very beholding of Christ is a transforming sight. The Spirit that makes us new creatures, and stirs us up to behold this servant, it is a transforming beholding. . . . A man cannot look upon the love of God and of Christ in the gospel, but it will change him to be like God and Christ. For how can we see Christ, and God in Christ, but we shall see how God hates sin, and this will transform us to hate it as God doth, who hated it so that it could not be expiated but with the blood of Christ, God-man. So, seeing the holiness of God in it, it will transform us to be holy. When we see the love of God in the gospel, and the love of Christ giving himself for us, this will transform us to love God.[6]

[6]Richard Sibbes, "A Description of Christ," in *The Works of Richard Sibbes* (Edinburgh: James Nichol, 1862-1864), 1:14.

My new life began when the Spirit first opened my eyes (there's the light) and won my heart (there's the heat) to Christ. Then, for the first time, I began to enjoy and love Christ as the Father has always done. And through Christ, for the first time, I began to enjoy and love the Father as the Son has always done. That was how it started, and that is how the new life goes on: by revealing the beauty, love, glory and kindness of Christ to me, the Spirit kindles in me an ever deeper and more sincere love for God. And as he stirs me to think ever more on Christ, he makes me more and more Godlike: less self-obsessed and more Christ-obsessed.

"Beauty's Self and Beauty's Giver"

The sinful turn from being lovers of God to being lovers of self of course makes us ever more devilishly ugly, ever more self-absorbed and vicious. But by cultivating in us a deepening taste for Christ, the epitome of beauty, the Spirit polishes a new humanity who begins to shine with his likeness. We become like what we worship. And, ultimately, that all applies even to our bodies: the turn from God in Genesis 3 meant a fall into physical decay, rot and death; but all of that will be more than undone by the Spirit, who will transform our moldering bodies to be like Christ's glorious, resurrection body (Phil 3:21; 1 Cor 15:44-49). The Spirit beautifies his new creation.

That means untwisting me. Naturally I am bent in on myself and I take a hellish delight in my own supposed independence. But if I am to be anything like the outgoing and outward-looking Father, Son and Spirit, the Spirit must take my eyes off myself (which he does by winning me to Christ). Of course, if God himself was not outward-looking, the Spirit would not need to bother—and he almost certainly wouldn't. If God only wanted me to live under his government, then the Spirit—if he could be bothered—would be more concerned simply to help me be a law-abiding citizen. My self-love need never be challenged. In

fact, I could nurture it very happily by fixating on just how well
I am keeping the rules. But the Spirit comes with a far deeper
purpose: that I might know the Son, and that I might be like
him—meaning that the whole point is that my eyes look out to
him. Knowing him is life, and looking to him is what enlivens.
Realizing this, said Charles Spurgeon, is the secret to Christian
happiness:

> It is ever the Holy Spirit's work to turn our eyes away from
> self to Jesus; but Satan's work is just the opposite of this, for
> he is constantly trying to make us regard ourselves instead
> of Christ. . . . We shall never find happiness by looking at
> our prayers, our doings, or our feelings; it is what *Jesus* is, not
> what we are, that gives rest to the soul. If we would at once
> overcome Satan and have peace with God, it must be by
> "looking unto Jesus."[7]

Life in the Trinity

Through the giving of the Spirit, God shares with us—and catches
us up into—the life that is his. The Father has eternally known
and loved his great Son, and through the Spirit he opens our eyes
that we too might know him, and so he wins our hearts that we
too might love him. Our love for the Son, then, is an echo and an
extension of the Father's eternal love. In other words, through the
Spirit the Father allows us to share in the enjoyment of what most
delights him—his Son. It was his overwhelming love for the Son
that inspired him to create us in the first place, and all so that we
might share in that highest pleasure of his.

This, in fact, is the heartbeat of what it means to be godly, to
be like this God. It is why Jesus says: "If God were your Father,
you would love me" (Jn 8:42). The Father's very identity consists

---

[7]Charles Spurgeon, "Morning, June 28," in *Morning and Evening* (Grand Rapids:
Zondervan, 1956).

in his love for the Son, and so when we love the Son we reflect what is most characteristic about the Father. It is the prime reason the Spirit is given. The Puritan theologian John Owen wrote that "therein consists the principal part of our renovation into his image. Nothing renders us so like unto God as our love unto Jesus Christ."[8]

But the Spirit not only enables us to know and love Christ; he also gives us the mind of Christ, making us like him. Now before anything else, what is most characteristic of the Son is his relationship with his Father, that he knows and enjoys receiving the love and life of the Father, "that I love the Father and that I do exactly what my

The return of the prodigal son

Father has commanded me" (Jn 14:31). At the heart of our transformation into the likeness of the Son, then, is our sharing of his deep delight in the Father. In our love and enjoyment of the Son we are like the Father; in our love and enjoyment of the Father we are like the Son. That is the happy life the Spirit calls us to.

We saw in the last chapter that it is the Spirit who unites us to Christ. Like the oil flowing down onto the body of the high priest, he imparts the blessings of Christ the Head to his Body, the church. He takes what is Christ's and makes it ours (Jn 16:14) so that in the beloved Son we might be the beloved children of God. How great and lovely, then, is the work of the Spirit! He unites us to the Son so that the Father's love for the Son also encompasses

[8]John Owen, "Christologia," in *The Works of John Owen,* ed. William H. Goold, 24 vols. (1850-1855; republished, Edinburgh: Banner of Truth, 1965-1991), 1:146.

us; he draws us to share the Father's own enjoyment of the Son; and he causes us to share the Son's delight in the Father. What could be more delicious than to keep in step with a Spirit whose purpose is that?

Jonathan Edwards wrote that "the divine principle in the saints is of the nature of the Spirit: for as the nature of the Spirit of God is divine love, so divine love is the nature and essence of that holy principle in the hearts of the saints."[9]

It is by the Spirit that the Father has eternally loved his Son. And so, by sharing their Spirit with us, the Father and the Son share with us their own life, love and fellowship. By the Spirit uniting me to Christ, the Father knows and loves me as his son; by the Spirit I begin to know and love him as my Father. By the Spirit I begin to love aright—unbending me from my self-love, he wins me to share the Father's pleasure in the Son and the Son's in the Father. By the Spirit I (slowly!) begin to love as God loves, with his own generous, overflowing, self-giving love for others.

KNOWING AND PRAYING TO THE FATHER, SON AND SPIRIT

One of the most insightful books on what it means to know the Father, Son and Spirit was written by the great seventeenth-century Puritan theologian John Owen. He gave it the snappy little title *Communion with God the Father, Son and Holy Ghost, Each Person Distinctly, in Love, Grace, and Consolation* (book titles were like that then).

He put it like that because he wanted to be very clear that there is no "God-in-general" or abstract Godhead for us to have fellowship with or to pray to. Christians are brought to have communion with the Father, communion with the Son and communion with the Spirit.

He starts with our communion with the Father, and what he says is especially touching because of how sensitive he is to the way we so easily shy away from the Father, as though he were all dark and

---

[9]Edwards, "Writings on the Trinity, Grace, and Faith," in *Works,* 21:191.

distant. "But just remember," Owen says in effect, "he is our most loving *Father.*"

> Every other discovery of God, without this, will but make the soul fly from him; but if the heart be once much taken up with this the eminency of the Father's love, it cannot choose but be overpowered, conquered, and endeared unto him. This, if any thing, will work upon us to make our abode with him. If the love of a father will not make a child delight in him, what will? Put, then, this to the venture: exercise your thoughts upon this very thing, the eternal, free, and fruitful love of the Father, and see if your hearts be not wrought upon to delight in him.[a]

The Father is the source of all the love we see in Christ, and so we are not to think of him as aloof and uncaring. In fact, Owen argued, the greatest unkindness you can do to him is to refuse to believe that he loves you: "You can no way more trouble or burden him."[b] He has adopted us and is our Father.

Next, the Son both perfectly reveals the Father to us and, by his life, death, resurrection and ascension, brings us to enjoy him as *our* Father. The Son, then, is the revealer and mediator, through whom we have communion with the Father. He is also the church's bridegroom, and rejoices not only to bring his bride to his Father, but also to know sweet communion with her himself.

John Owen (1616-1683) with—as was said at the time—"as much powder in his hair as would discharge eight cannons."

Then, the Spirit comforts us. Where our sin makes us prone to doubt, anxiety and cold-heartedness, where Satan buffets us with accusations, the Spirit brings assurance of the Father's love and the Son's perfect salvation. He makes communion with the Son and the Father both real and delightful. "And this is his work to the end of the world,—to bring the promises of Christ to our minds and hearts, to give us the comfort of them, the joy and sweetness of them."[c]

What does it all mean for how we pray? Well, since we have communion with all three persons, it is quite right that we should pray to all three: Jesus commends prayer to the Father (Jn 16:23); Stephen prayed to Jesus in Acts 7:59; and while it is harder to find clear instances in the Bible of prayer to the Spirit, Owen is adamant that we can: "The Holy Ghost, being God, is no less to be invocated, prayed to, and called on, than the Father and Son."[d]

That said, *normal* Christian prayer is something richer and juicier: we join in with the fellowship as the Father, Son and Spirit are already enjoying it. That is, the Son—who is already interceding for us with his Father—brings us to be with him before his Father. Think of the high priest going into the presence of the Lord in the holy of holies: just so the Son takes us before his Father—and there the Spirit helps us (Rom 8:26). And so the Spirit supports us, the Son brings us and the Father—who always delights to hear the prayers of his Son—hears us with joy. With the Son, secure in him, enabled as he is by the Spirit, we pray to our Father.

Now, to pray like this—to pray "Abba" in Jesus' name, empowered by the Spirit—isn't just the flashy Christian's way of showing off his theological virtuosity; it is to revel in the shape of God's own fellowship and beauty. Think how different it would be if God were not like this: if the Spirit did not make us cry "Abba" because God is not really a Father and has no Beloved beside him. Could such a single-person God even hear us from all the way up there in his self-involved transcendence? Wouldn't our bleating just be an interruption on his precious me-time? Yes, if God were not triune, it would probably be better to keep quiet and hope to avoid being heard. After all, he may not want the existence of anything else.

---

[a]Owen, "Communion with God," in Works, 2:36.
[b]Ibid., 2:21.
[c]Ibid., 2:237.
[d]Ibid., 2:229-30.

"True Religion, in Great Part, Consists In . . ."

Everything we have seen means that life with this God is as different from life with any other God as oranges are from orangutans. If, for example, God weren't about having us know and love him, but simply about having us live under his rule, then our behavior and performance would be all that mattered. The deeper, internal questions of what we want, what we love and enjoy would never be asked. As it is, because the Christian life is one of being brought to share the delight the Father, Son and Spirit have for each other, *desires matter*. As Jonathan Edwards put it, "True religion, in great part, consists in holy affections."[10] He was thinking primarily of love for Christ and joy in him, and he wrote one of his main works *(Religious Affections)* largely to unpack that conviction.

What Edwards was getting at was the fact that the Spirit is not about bringing us to a mere external performance for Christ, but bringing us actually to love him and find our joy in him. And any performance "for him" that is not the expression of such love brings him no pleasure at all. Edwards compares such loveless Christianity to a cold marriage, asking:

> If a wife should carry it [that is, behave] very well to her husband, and not at all from any love to him, but from other considerations plainly seen, and certainly known by the husband, would he at all delight in her outward respect any more than if a wooden image were contrived to make respectful motions in his presence?[11]

"Of course not!" is what Edwards expects us to chuckle.

What we love and enjoy is foundationally important. It is far more significant than our outward behavior, for it is our desires that *drive* our behavior. We do what we want. The Father, Son and Spirit love and enjoy each other and, created in their image, we

---

[10]Edwards, "Religious Affections," in *Works,* 2:95.
[11]Edwards, "Writings on the Trinity, Grace, and Faith," in *Works,* 21:172.

"THE EXPULSIVE POWER OF A NEW AFFECTION"

Thomas Chalmers (1780-1847) started out as one of those clergymen who don't really care. In fact, he was explicit in his belief that the duties of his parish of Kilmany (near St. Andrews in Scotland) really ought not take up more than one day a week. Then, aged twenty-nine, he fell dangerously ill and was confined to bed with the works of evangelicals such as William Wilberforce.

Thomas Chalmers

When he arose, it was as a new man, eager to preach salvation through grace alone, and large crowds were soon descending on Kilmany to hear him. Four years later, in 1815, he moved to the Tron Church in Glasgow, and word spread through the country of this "living fire" in the pulpit. "All the world wild about Chalmers," wrote Wilberforce in his diary—and he was not exaggerating: thousands came to hear his broad Fife tones; one time, Chalmers could only get into the church through a window.

were made to love and enjoy them. Blindly and foolishly, though, we have all turned to love and enjoy other things—things that in reality are completely unable to satisfy. But the Spirit's first work is to set our desires in order, to open our eyes and give us the Father's own relish for the Son, and the Son's own enjoyment of the Father.

The Heidelberg Catechism (1563) captures this brilliantly when it asks: "What is the coming-to-life of the new man?"

He would go on later to professorships at the universities of St. Andrews and Edinburgh—and would lead the formation of the Free Church of Scotland—but it was in those Glasgow years that he gave a sermon that explained what his preaching was now about, and how we are to walk in the Spirit. The sermon was based on 1 John 2:15 and titled "The Expulsive Power of a New Affection."

Our problem, he explained, is that naturally our lives are guided and controlled by a love for "the world." What can we do? Resolve to do better? Try to convince ourselves that the world is not really so alluring after all? No, he said, that "is altogether incompetent and ineffectual," for nobody can "dispossess the heart of an old affection, but by the expulsive power of a new one." We cannot choose *what* we love, but always love what seems desirable to us. Thus we will only change what we love when something proves itself to be more desirable to us than what we already love. I will, then, always love sin and the world until I truly sense that Christ is better.

And this is what the Spirit does in us: he makes us taste and see that the Lord is good, supremely good, and thus he causes us to desire him: "He, the God of love, so sets Himself forth in characters of endearment, that nought but faith, and nought but understanding, are wanting, on your part, to call forth the love of your hearts back again."[a]

It was how Chalmers wielded the sword of the Spirit: he made Christ known that hearts might be won.

[a]Thomas Chalmers, *The Works of Thomas Chalmers* (Bridgeport: M. Sherman, 1829), 3:64.

Answer: "It is wholehearted joy in God through Christ and a delight to do every kind of good as God wants us to."[12]

The Spirit of the Father and the Son would never be interested in merely empowering us to "do good." His desire (which is the desire of the Father and the Son) is to bring us to such a hearty enjoyment of God through Christ that we delight to know him,

[12]Christian Reformed Church, *Ecumenical Creeds and Reformed Confessions* (Grand Rapids: Faith Alive Christian Resources, 1988), p. 54.

that we delight in all his ways, and that *therefore* we want to do as he wants and we hate the thought of ever grieving him.

Stripped-Down Salvation

What a life the Spirit gives! He gives us himself, opening up to us the lovely fellowship of Father, Son and Spirit; and he wins our hearts to share their satisfaction and pleasure in each other. Who, knowing this, could ever prefer the "cleaner," leaner idea of a single-person God? For, strip down God and make him lean and you must strip down his salvation and make it mean. Instead of a life bursting with love, joy and fellowship, all you will be left with is the watery gruel of religion. Instead of a loving Father, a distant potentate; instead of fellowship, contract. No security in the beloved Son, no heart-change, no joy in God could that spirit bring.

Far, far from theological clutter, God's being Father, Son and Spirit is just what makes the Christian life beautiful.

The Family of Heaven

One of the key ingredients to that beauty is how friendly and familial it all is. God the Father enjoys being himself: he enjoys his Son, he enjoys being a Father to him, and all so much that he chose to share his Fatherliness and fellowship with those he would create. And so, when this God created, he "created man in his own image, in the image of God he created him; *male and female* he created them" (Gen 1:27). Loving familial relationship, this God makes a man and a woman, a husband and a wife; he creates a family and makes people designed for fellowship with each other. As the Father, Son and Spirit have always known fellowship with each other, so we in the image of God are made for fellowship.

Now of course we haven't and don't tend to value fellowship—or at least, not as highly as we value getting our own way. When Adam and Eve turned in on themselves in self-love in Genesis 3, they not only turned away from the Lord God; they turned away from each other. Thus, not only did their relationship with the Lord break down, their relationship with each other broke down: ashamed of their open nakedness before one another, they hide behind fig leaves and begin to cast blame. And before long, Cain is killing Abel, Lamech is dreaming of vengeance, and the human family is torn apart by lovelessness and malice.

But the triune God's delight in family still stands. And so the Father sends the Son, not only to reconcile us to himself, but to reconcile us to each other in order that the world might be a place of harmony, reflecting their harmony. The Son's purpose, wrote Paul,

> was to create in himself one new man out of the two [Jew and Gentile], thus making peace, and in this one body to reconcile both of them to God through the cross, by which he put to death their hostility. He came and preached peace to you who were far away and peace to those who were near. For through him we both have access to the Father by one Spirit. (Eph 2:15-18)

The Spirit wins male and female, black and white, Jew and Gentile all to the same uniting love of God which spills over into a heartfelt love of one another. He unites us to the Son so that together we cry "Abba" and begin to know each other truly as brothers and sisters. For the new humanity is a new family; it is the spreading family of the Father.

At the heart of Jesus' high priestly prayer to his Father for believers is the request "that they may be one as we are one" (Jn 17:22). That is not the sort of request one could put to a single-person God. Such a God would, of course, like oneness—after all, he is One—but it would be a very different sort of oneness from what Jesus has in mind.

Oneness for the single-person God would mean *sameness*. Alone for eternity without any beside him, why would he value others and their differences? Think how it works out for Allah:

under his influence, the once-diverse cultures of Nigeria, Persia and Indonesia are made, deliberately and increasingly, *the same*. Islam presents a complete way of life for individuals, nations and cultures, binding them into one way of praying, one way of marrying, buying, fighting, relating—even, some would say, one way of eating and dressing.

Oneness for the triune God means *unity*. As the Father is absolutely one with his Son, and yet is not his Son, so Jesus prays that believers might be one, but not that they might all be the same. Created male *and* female, in the image of this God, and with many other good differences between us, we come together valuing the way the triune God has made us each unique.

> There are different kinds of gifts, but the same Spirit. . . . If the whole body were an eye, where would the sense of hearing be? If the whole body were an ear, where would the sense of smell be? But in fact God has arranged the parts in the body, every one of them, just as he wanted them to be. If they were all one part, where would the body be? As it is, there are many parts, but one body. (1 Cor 12:4, 17-20)

So it is not just that the Father, Son and Spirit call us into fellowship with themselves; they share their heavenly harmony that there might be harmony on earth, that people of different genders, languages, hobbies and gifts might be one in peace and love; and that one day, with one heart and one voice, we might cry: "Salvation belongs to our God, who sits on the throne, and to the Lamb" (Rev 7:10). And that is what the family of God—by its very existence—makes known to the world: that the God of harmony is *the* hope for world peace; that he can and will unite enemies, rivals and strangers into one loving family under his fatherly care.

Onward and Outward

Now some families like to keep themselves to themselves, but not this one. No, the outgoing Father, that original fountain of all life and love, is the head of an outgoing family. His life and being is one of going out with his love, and that is the life his children are brought to share.

A good road into this starts with Jesus' first words to his friends after the resurrection. On the evening of the first Easter day, Jesus came to his disciples and said: "'Peace be with you! As the Father has sent me, I am sending you.' And with that he breathed on them and said, 'Receive the Holy Spirit'" (Jn 20:21-22).

The disciples should not have been at all surprised. Jesus had told them he would be resurrected, and he had told them that "whatever the Father does the Son also does" (Jn 5:19). The first thing the Father does, of course, is love the Son, breathing out his Spirit on him. Just so, doing as his Father does, Jesus breathes out the Spirit on his disciples. In fact, he had already said to them: "As the Father has loved me, so have I loved you" (Jn 15:9). But the Father also *sends* the Son; and doing as his Father does, Jesus thus sends his disciples. Like Father, like Son.

That entirely changes what mission looks like. For it is not, then, that God lounges back in heaven, simply phoning in his order that we get on with evangelism so that he might get more servants. If that were the case, evangelism would take *a lot* of self-motivation—and you can always tell when the church thinks like that, for that's when evangelism gets left to the more adrenaline-stoked salespeople/professionals. But the reality is so different. The truth is that God is *already* on mission: in love, the Father has sent his Son and his Spirit. It is the outworking of his very nature.

That means that when we go out and share the knowledge of God's great love we reflect something very profound about who God is. For when Jesus sends us, he is allowing us to *share* the missional, generous, outgoing shape of God's own life. The writer of Hebrews puts it like this: "Jesus also suffered outside the city gate [that is, he went out beyond where the people of God are] to make the people holy through his own blood. *Let us, then, go to him* outside the camp" (Heb 13:12-13). In other words, Jesus is found *out there,* in the place of rejection. That is where the Father has sent him, that he might bring sinners back as children. The Christian life is one of being where he is, of joining in how he has been sent.

And the motivation? Well, why did the Father send the Son? Because the Father so enjoyed loving the Son that he wanted his love to be in others. John 17:25-26 says: "Righteous Father, though the world does not know you, I know you, and they know that *you have sent me.* I have made you known to them, and will continue to make you known in order *that the love you have for me may be in them and that I myself may be in them.*"

And why did the Son go? Because, he says, "I love the Father and . . . I do exactly what my Father has commanded me" (Jn 14:31). So the Father sent the Son because of how he so loved him (and wanted that love to be shared and enjoyed), and the Son went because he so loved his Father (and wanted *that* love to be shared and enjoyed). The mission comes from the overflow of love, from the uncontainable enjoyment of the fellowship.

So it is with the Father and the Son; so it is with us. The Spirit catches us up to share their pleasure, and it is that delight in them that fuels us to *want* to make them known. The Spirit-caused enjoyment of the fellowship, the increasing love for the Father and the Son: it turns us to share their outgoing love for the world. We become like what we worship.

The Puritan Richard Sibbes once said that a Christian singing God's praises to the world is like a bird singing. Birds sing loudest, he said, when the sun rises and warms them; and so it is with Christians: when they are warmed by the Light of the world, by the love of God in Christ, that is when they sing loudest.

As the shining of the sun enlargeth the spirit of the poor

creatures, the birds, in the spring time, to sing, so proportionably the apprehension of the sweet love of God in Christ enlargeth the spirit of a man, and makes him full of joy and thanksgiving. He breaks forth into joy, so that his whole life is matter of joy and thanksgiving.[13]

Sibbes was quite right, for "out of the overflow of the heart the mouth speaks" (Mt 12:34). If I don't enjoy Christ, I won't speak of him. Or, perhaps worse, I will, but without love and enjoyment—and if my mouth does give away my heart, people will hear of an unwanted Christ. And who would want that?

The Spirit, of course, *can* use such loveless evangelism. But his real work is to bring us to, and keep us in, the sunshine of God's love. It is there that we will sing heartily; it is there, abiding in Christ, that we will bear fruit. The Spirit shares the triune life of God by bringing God's children into the mutual delight of the Father and the Son—and there we become like our God: fruitful and life-giving.

---

[13]Sibbes, "The Matchless Love and Inbeing," in *Works*, 6:388.

"Who Among the Gods
Is Like You, O LORD?"

How the Atheists Are Right

For the last two hundred years or so, atheism in the West has been marching forward with ever more confidence and power. Its cries have not only heartened the person on the street who would simply rather do without God and religion; they have also inspired a new, ultra-aggressive squad of "antitheists." Leaping past the frontline argument that there is no God, these antitheists have pushed on to argue that even *were* God to exist, that would be a Bad Thing. Belief in God is not so much like the child's comfort blanket; it is like the child's nightmare.

Why? The argument is both fascinating and deeply revealing. Christopher Hitchens, author of *God Is Not Great*—and one of the four horsemen of the militant "New Atheism"—put it like this:

> I think it would be rather awful if it was true. If there was a permanent, total, round-the-clock divine supervision and invigilation of everything you did, you would never have a waking or sleeping moment when you weren't being watched and controlled and supervised by some celestial entity from the moment of your conception to the moment of your death. . . . It would be like living in North Korea.[1]

---

[1]Christopher Hitchens, interview on *Hannity & Colmes*, Fox News, May 13, 2007.

For Hitchens, God is The Ruler, and so must by definition be a Stalin-in-the-sky, a Big Brother. And who in their right mind would ever want such a being to exist? In other words, the anti-theist's problem is not so much with the *existence* of God as with the *character* of God. He will write and fight against the existence of God because he is repelled by the thought of *that* sort of being. *That* God is not great.

But the triune God is not that God. Hitchens, clearly, had it in his head that God is *fundamentally* The Ruler, The One in Charge, characterized by "supervision and invigilation." The picture changes entirely, though, if God is *fundamentally* the most kind and loving Father, and only ever exercises his rule *as who he is—* as a Father. In that case, living under his roof is not like living in North Korea at all, but like living in the household of the sort of caring father Hitchens himself wished for.

Friedrich Schleiermacher
(1768-1834)

Is it too much of a coincidence that the advance of atheism parallels the retreat of the church on the Trinity? The nineteenth century was the century where Marx dismissed religion as "the opium of the people" and where Nietzsche declared: "God is dead." And it was the century that opened with its perhaps most eminent theologian, Friedrich Schleiermacher, making the Trinity a mere appendix to the Christian faith; it was the century that closed with his greatest successor, Adolf von Harnack, dismissing the Trinity altogether as a bundle of philosophical rot. Of course, the theologians weren't feeding the atheists, but they were disarming the church so that the atheists could storm on without meeting much serious opposition. For if God is not a Father, if he has no Son and will have no children, then he must be lonely, distant and unapproachable; if he is not triune and so not essentially loving, then no God at all just looks better.

The atheists are not alone in this. The popular turn to various alternative spiritualities—from New Age and neopaganism to Wicca and plain old superstition—is routinely connected with a dislike for the idea of a personal God. For surely, isn't such a being at best a monstrous bore and at worst something much, much darker? In my own experience, talking with non-Christian students, again and again I find that when they describe the God they don't believe in, he sounds more like Satan than the loving Father of Jesus Christ: greedy, selfish, trigger-happy and entirely devoid of love. And if God is not Father, Son and Spirit, aren't they right?

Israel's Alternative

But how radically and overwhelmingly different is the God of the Bible! Not needy, solitary and selfish, but bountiful, loving and self-giving at the very heart of who he is. Karl Barth wrote:

> The triunity of God is the secret of His beauty. If we deny this, we at once have a God without radiance and without joy (and without humour!); a God without beauty. Losing the dignity and power of real divinity, He also loses His beauty. But if we keep to this . . . that the one God is Father, Son and Holy Spirit, we cannot escape the fact either in general or in detail that apart from anything else God is also beautiful.[2]

If God is not Father, Son and Spirit, then he is eminently rejectable:

---

[2]Karl Barth, *Church Dogmatics* II/1, ed. G. W. Bromiley and T. F. Torrance (Edinburgh: T & T Clark, 1936-1977), p. 661.

without love, radiance or beauty. Who would want such a God to have any power, or even to exist? But the triune, living God of the Bible is Beauty. Here is a God we can really *want*, and whose sovereignty we can wholeheartedly rejoice in.

Colin Gunton, who until his tragic death a few years ago was professor of Christian doctrine at King's College London, summed up one of the key differences the Trinity makes like this: "Prominent among the attributes [that is, divine characteristics] we have encountered has been that of the divine mercy, which would rarely appear high up the list of attributes in a 'natural' account of the divine. . . . Mercy is the outworking in fallen time and history of the action of a God for whom love of the other is central to his being."[3]

That is, if God were not personal, he could not be merciful (*things* do not show mercy); but if God were just *one* person, then love of the other would not be central to his being. There would have been nobody in eternity for him to love. Thus the only God inherently inclined to show mercy is the Father who has eternally loved his Son by the Spirit. Only with this God do such winning qualities as love and mercy rank highly.

It is crucially important, then, that Christians be clear and specific about which God we believe in. We must not be heard to believe in just any "God," but in *this* God. Today that seems especially vital. And it is not just for the sake of unbelievers. John Calvin said that the sinful human mind is like "a perpetual factory of idols,"[4] meaning that we are all constantly distorting the nature of God in our minds, making the Father of lights out to be less than he is, and devilish. In fact, this tendency is the very source of all spiritual coldness, for when we suspect that God is really a Stalin-in-the-sky, of course we run from him.

---

[3]Colin Gunton, *The Christian Faith: An Introduction to Christian Doctrine* (Oxford: Blackwell, 2001), p. 188.
[4]John Calvin, *Institutes of the Christian Religion* 1.11.8.

We have a real challenge here, for it is very easy to speak about some "God-in-general," perhaps as if there were some "God" behind and before Father, Son and Spirit. We can do a lot of such "God-talk," even speaking about God's constancy, glory, sovereignty and so on, and *still* not be clear which God we are talking about. The single-person God could be described as glorious, constant and powerful, but all such characteristics, when characteristics of *that* God, would be horrifying. Is he constant in his lovelessness? To what end does he use his frightful power? And what exactly is *his* glory?

But the triune being of God changes the flavor and meaning of every word we use about him. His glory, for example, is entirely different than the glory of any other god; his power and justice quite unique. In fact, when we speak of God's characteristics—God's majesty, say—and we are clear that we are referring to the majesty of the Father, Son and Spirit, then God's majesty shows itself to be something infinitely more beautiful than we could otherwise have seen. Of course, for now we have distinguished the majesty of the living God from the majesty of idols.

Let us take God's majesty as an example. If Aristotle's God, the "Unmoved Mover," were God, then his majesty would be entirely and only forbidding. Aristotle believed that the perfection of God's majesty means that everything else is beneath his consideration. Why would God ever think about anything else, when he has his own perfect majesty to contemplate? His majesty would mean our consignment to irrelevance for him.

But if God is an *outgoing* God, if fundamentally he is a life-giving Father for whom "love of the other is central to his being," then his majesty must be outgoing. And that is just what we see in Scripture: God's majesty is displayed when he goes out and acts, when he saves his people and shakes evil from the earth. *His* majesty is a loving majesty. Consider the clash of images in Psalm 113: "Who is like the Lord our God, the One who sits enthroned on high, who stoops down to look on the heavens and the earth? He raises the poor from the dust and lifts the needy from the ash heap" (Ps 113:5-7). Khaled Anatolios comments: "Compassion for the lowly, rather than self-absorbed contemplation, is the proper characteristic of divine majesty in the Hebrew scriptures."[5] Indeed, for such displays of compassion are the outworking of the eternal majesty of the Father in his love for his Son.

What I'd like to do with the rest of this chapter is to see how the triune being of God shapes some of the words we use about him. In other words, to see some of the differences the Trinity makes to how we think about God. And through it all, I'll be turning especially to Jonathan Edwards for help: in this area, as in many areas, he is, I have found, uncannily far-seeing, clear and, yes, helpful. Now we use a lot of words to describe God, and I don't want to turn this into a hulking beast of a book, so we'll just get a taste, as it were, and look at three pivotal areas: God's holiness, God's wrath and God's glory. How does the Trinity brighten and define them?

The Highest Beauty

First up: God's holiness. "Oh dear!" you might sigh—and I'd understand, for without the Trinity, holiness does have the smell of mothballs about it, the look of a Victorian matron administering castor oil. And much of what purports to be holiness has just that aura about it: all prickliness and prudery. People even say things like, "Yes, God is loving, but he is *also* holy"—as if holiness is an unloving thing, the cold side of God that stops God from being *too* loving.

Balderdash! Poppycock! Or at least, it is if you are talking about the holiness of the Father, Son and Spirit. No, said Jonathan Edwards:

---

[5]Khaled Anatolios, *Athanasius: The Coherence of His Thought* (London and New York: Routledge, 1998), p. 14.

Holiness is a most beautiful, lovely thing. Men are apt to drink in strange notions of holiness from their childhood, as if it were a melancholy, morose, sour, and unpleasant thing; but there is nothing in it but what is sweet and ravishingly lovely. 'Tis the highest beauty and amiableness, vastly above all other beauties; 'tis a divine beauty.[6]

What is holiness, then? The words used for holiness in the Bible have the basic meaning of being "set apart." But there our troubles begin, because naturally I think I'm lovely. So if God is "set apart" from me, I assume the problem is with him (and I can do all this in the subtlest, most subconscious way). His holiness looks like a prissy rejection of my happy, healthy loveliness.

Dare I burst my own bubble now? I must. For the reality is that *I* am the cold, selfish, vicious one, full of darkness and dirtiness. And God is holy—"set apart" from me—precisely in that he is *not* like that. He is not set apart from us in priggishness, but by the fact that there are no such ugly traits in him as there are in us. "God is God," wrote Edwards, "and distinguished from [that is, set apart from] all other beings, and exalted above 'em, *chiefly by his divine beauty*" (for the connection between holiness and beauty, see verses like Psalm 96:9).[7]

Now the holiness of a single-person God would be something quite different. His holiness would be about being set apart *away from others.* In other words, his holiness would be all about aloof distance. But the holiness of the Father, Son and Spirit is all about love. Given who this God is, it must be. Edwards again: "Both the holiness and happiness of the Godhead consists in this love. As we have already proved, all creature holiness consists essentially and summarily in love to God and love to other creatures; *so does*

---

[6]Jonathan Edwards, "Sermons and Discourses, 1720-1723," in *The Works of Jonathan Edwards,* ed. Wilson H. Kimnach (New Haven and London: Yale University Press, 1957-2008), 10:478.
[7]Edwards, "Religious Affections," in *Works,* 2:298, my emphasis.

the holiness of God consist in his love, especially in the perfect and intimate union and love there is between the Father and the Son."[8]

The holiness of the triune God is the perfection, beauty and absolute purity of the love there is between the Father and the Son. There is nothing grubby or abusive about the love of this God—and *thus* he is holy. My love is naturally all perverse and misdirected; but his love is set apart from mine in perfection. And so, the holiness of the triune God does not moderate or cool his love; his holiness is the lucidity and spotlessness of his overflowing love.

How to be Thor-like

It all dramatically affects what it means for the believer to be holy, to be godly—in other words, what it means to be *like* God. Being like another God would look quite different. If God is a being curved in on himself, then to be like him I should be like that. If Aristotle's eternally introspective God is God, then plenty of navel-gazing seems to be just what's called for. For what we think God is like must shape our godliness, and what we think godliness is reveals what we think of God. So, what, for example, if love and relationship were not central to God's being? Then they wouldn't feature for me either as I sought to grow in God-likeness. Forget others. If God is all single and solitary, be a hermit. If God is cruel and haughty, be cruel and haughty. If God is the sort of oversexed, beer-sloshing war-god beloved of the Vikings, be like that. (Though please don't.)

But with this God, no wonder the two greatest commands are

---

[8]Edwards, "Writings on the Trinity, Grace, and Faith," in *Works*, 21:186, my emphasis.

"Love the Lord your God" and "Love your neighbor as yourself." For *that* is being like this God—sharing the love the Father and the Son have for each other, and then, like them, overflowing with that love to the world. Or look, for example, at Leviticus 19, where the Lord famously says, "Be holy because I, the Lord your God, am holy" (Lev 19:2). What does holiness look like there? It means not turning to idols but coming to the Lord with proper fellowship offerings (Lev 19:4-8). That is, it means fellowship with the Lord. And it means not being mean to the poor, not lying, not stealing, and so on (Lev 19:10-16)—that is, it means: "Do not hate your brother in your heart . . . but love your neighbor as yourself" (Lev 19:17-18). Love for the Lord, love for neighbor—that is the heart of holiness and how the triune God's people get to be like him.

The beautiful, loving holiness of this God makes true godliness a warm, attractive, delightful thing. It is not about becoming more mean and pinched, for this God is not mean and pinched. Holiness for God, said Edwards, "is as it were the beauty and sweetness of the divine nature," and so "Christians that shine by reflecting the light of the Sun of Righteousness, do shine with the same sort of brightness, the same mild, sweet and pleasant beams."[9] And most essentially, to know and enjoy the God who is love means becoming, like him, loving. "Dear friends, let us love one another, for love comes from God. Everyone who loves has been born of God and knows God. Whoever does not love does not know God, because God is love" (1 Jn 4:7-8).

When Love Meets Evil

Now if God's holiness can seem off-putting, his wrath can seem hideous. And if God is not triune, it is. If God is just the biggest boy in the school who must have his every way or else lose it in fits of carpet-biting rage, then his anger is repellent. All his other good

---

[9]Edwards, "Religious Affections," in *Works*, 2:201, 347.

qualities would be as nothing when we saw those red eyes. Yet that is just how God's anger is often seen. Commenting on Romans 1:18 ("The wrath of God is being revealed from heaven against all the godlessness and wickedness of men"), New Testament scholar Stephen Moore writes: "We can almost hear the bones cracking on the wheel as the might of the offended sovereign bears down upon the body of the condemned."[10]

But. In fact, let me say that again: *But*. However it might be with other gods, that is just not how it is with the Father, Son and Spirit. With this God, it is not as if sometimes he *has* love and sometimes he *has* wrath, as if those are different moods so that when he's feeling one he's not feeling the other. No, for all eternity the Father was loving his Son, but never once was he angry. Why? Because there was nothing to be angry with until Adam sinned in Genesis 3. So God's anger at evil from Genesis 3 onward is a *new* thing: it is how the God who is love responds to evil.

Like God's holiness, then, his wrath is not something that sits awkwardly next to his love. Nor is it something unrelated to his love. God is angry at evil *because* he loves. Isaiah speaks of the pouring out of God's wrath as his "*strange* work," his "*alien* task" (Is 28:21), because it is not that God is naturally angry, but that evil provokes him: in his pure love, God cannot tolerate evil. That makes complete sense to me as a father: if I could twiddle my thumbs and yawn while my daughters suffered, it would prove I didn't really love them; but precisely *because* I so love them I hate the thought of anything evil befalling them. How much more is it so with the Father of lights, in whom there is no darkness at all. Love cares, and that means it cannot be indifferent to evil. "*Love* must be sincere. *Hate* what is evil; cling to what is good" (Rom 12:9). Only such love is sincere.

Croatian theologian Miroslav Volf has described how it took

---

[10]Stephen Moore, *God's Gym* (New York and London: Routledge, 1996), p. 17.

the horrors of ethnic warfare happening around him to appreciate the goodness of God's wrath:

> I used to think that wrath was unworthy of God. Isn't God love? Shouldn't divine love be beyond wrath? God is love, and God loves every person and every creature. That's exactly why God is wrathful against some of them. My last resistance to the idea of God's wrath was a casualty of the war in the former Yugoslavia, the region from which I come. According to some estimates, 200,000 people were killed and over 3,000,000 were displaced. *My* villages and cities were destroyed, *my* people shelled day in and day out, some of them brutalized beyond imagination, and I could not imagine God not being angry. Or think of Rwanda in the last decade of the past century where 800,000 people were hacked to death in one hundred days! How did God react to the carnage? By doting on the perpetrators in a grandparently fashion? By refusing to condemn the bloodbath but instead affirming the perpetrators' basic goodness? Wasn't God fiercely angry with them? Though I used to complain about the indecency of the idea of God's wrath, I came to think that I would have to rebel against a God who wasn't wrathful at the sight of the world's evil. God isn't wrathful in spite of being love. God is wrathful *because* God is love.[11]

Were God not triune, and so not eternally love, his wrath would make him look like an overgrown, foot-stamping toddler, a fight-picking bully or a merciless sultan. Think of the hormonal outbursts of the gods of ancient Greece and Rome. But with the God who is eternally love, his anger must rise *from* that love. Thus his anger is holy, set apart from our temper-tantrums; it is how he in his love reacts to evil. The Father loves his Son, and so hates sin,

---

[11]Miroslav Volf, *Free of Charge: Giving and Forgiving in a Culture Stripped of Grace* (Grand Rapids: Zondervan, 2006), pp. 138-39.

"Let there be light!"

which ultimately is rejection of the Son; he loves his children, and so hates their being oppressed; he loves his world, and so hates all evil in it. Thus in his love he roots out sin in his people, even disciplining them that they might be freed from their captivity to it. In his love he is patient with us. And in his love he promises finally to destroy all evil as light destroys darkness.

The wrath of the triune God is exactly the opposite of a character blip or a nasty side in him. It is the proof of the sincerity of his love, *that he truly cares*. His love is not mild-mannered and limp; it is livid, potent and committed. And therein lies our hope: through his wrath the living God shows that he is truly loving, and through his wrath he will destroy all devilry that we might enjoy him in a purified world, the home of righteousness.

From Zion, Perfect in Beauty, God Shines Forth

Is God *really* impelled by love, though? Now after everything we have seen, that might sound a harebrained question. God is love; he showed his love by sending his Son; his desire was to share his love for the Son: what could be the problem? And yet there are verses that could feel like pebbles in the shoe here. Paul, for example, writes that the Father "has blessed us in the heavenly realms with every spiritual blessing in Christ . . . *in order that we, who were the first to hope in Christ, might be for the praise of his glory*" (Eph 1:3-12). Is there, then, some deeper and perhaps selfish motivation in God: not love, but a craving for applause?

It all depends on what "the glory of God" means. In the Old Testament, the word for "glory" has to do with "heaviness" or "weight." In 1 Samuel 4:18, for example, "Eli fell backwards off his chair by the side of the gate. His neck was broken and he died, for he was an old man and *heavy*." So the glory of something is its mass, its bulk, its worth, what makes it up, what it is all about—indeed, what makes it *itself*. Perhaps Eli's glory was his stomach. Someone else's glory might be his or her brain, job or looks, if that is what they most treasure. The glory of a man who lives for money is money—and so: "Do not be overawed when a man grows rich, when the splendor *[glory]* of his house increases; for he will take nothing with him when he dies, his splendor *[glory]* will not descend with him" (Ps 49:16-17). (The lesson being, have instead a Glory that will go through death with you, as the psalmist did: "But God will redeem my life from the grave; he will surely take me to himself" [v. 15].)

That all means that "glorifying" God cannot be about inflating, improving or expanding him. That is quite impossible with the God who is already superabundant and overflowing with life. Instead, when we give God the glory, we simply ascribe to him what is already his, declaring him to be as he truly is. "Ascribe to the LORD the glory *due to his name*," said David (Ps 29:2).

So what is the glory of this God, the triune God? What is it like? It will, of course, be a radically different sort of glory from that of any other god. This God is simply nothing like any others. The answer is surprising: Ezekiel 1 speaks of God's glory in terms of both a person *and* a light/radiance/brightness. Ezekiel writes of how, when standing by the Kebar River, he saw a throne approaching, carried by four great living creatures. On the throne "was a figure like that of a man," and "he looked like fire; and brilliant light surrounded him. Like the appearance of a rainbow in the clouds on a rainy day, so was the radiance around him. *This was the appearance of the likeness of the glory of the LORD*" (Ezek 1:26-28). The appearance of the glory looks like both a man and a brilliant light.

First of all, *the light*. You wouldn't expect God's weight to be described as being like light, but Ezekiel is simply recording something seen throughout the Bible: that God's glory—his nature and character—is like a pure and dazzling light radiating outward and shining forth. Here are just a few examples:

> Then the glory of the LORD rose from above the cherubim and moved to the threshold of the temple. The cloud filled the temple, and the court was full of *the radiance of the glory* of the LORD. (Ezek 10:4)

> I saw the glory of the God of Israel coming from the east. His voice was like the roar of rushing waters, and the land was *radiant with his glory*. (Ezek 43:2)

> *Arise, shine, for your light has come, and the glory of the LORD rises upon you*. See, darkness covers the earth and thick darkness is over the peoples, but *the LORD rises upon you and his glory appears over you*. (Is 60:1-2)

In Psalm 19, the heavens are said to "declare the glory of God. . . . Their voice goes out into all the earth, their words to the ends of the world." Then the psalmist gets specific: "In the heavens he has pitched a tent for the sun, which is like a bridegroom coming forth from his pavilion, like a champion rejoicing to run his course. It rises at one end of the heavens and makes its circuit to the other; nothing is hidden from its heat" (Ps 19:1-6). As the glory of the Lord rises and shines, driving away the thick darkness, so the sun rises and shines to fill the heavens and the earth with a taste of that glory.

> And there were shepherds living out in the fields nearby, keeping watch over their flocks at night. An angel of the Lord appeared to them, and *the glory of the Lord shone* around them. (Lk 2:8-9)

At Jesus' transfiguration, Peter and his companions "saw his glory" (Lk 9:32). And what did it look like? "His face shone like the sun, and his clothes became as white as the light" (Mt 17:2).

> The city does not need the sun or the moon to shine on it, for *the glory of God gives it light*, and the Lamb is its lamp. (Rev 21:23)

So the glory of God is like radiant light, shining out, enlightening and giving life. And that is what the innermost being and weight of God is like: he is a sun of light, life and warmth, always shining *out*. As the Father gives out life and being to the Son, as the Father and the Son breathe out the Spirit, so the Spirit breathes out life into the world. The glory of this God is radiant and outgoing. As the sun gives of its own light and heat, so this God glories in giving himself. Thus, wrote Jonathan Edwards: "What God has in view in neither of them, neither in his manifesting his glory to the understanding nor communication to the heart, is not that he may receive, but that he [may] go forth: the main end of his shining forth is not that he may have his rays reflected back to himself, but that the rays may go forth."[12]

In other words, the beautiful glory of the triune God is radiating, self-giving and loving. That is why, when commenting on the glory of Ezekiel 1 and its New Testament counterpart, Revelation 4–5, Edwards said,

> Christ in the gospel revelation appears as clothed with love, as being as it were on a throne of mercy and grace, a seat of love encompassed about with pleasant beams of love. Love is the light and glory which are about the throne on which God sits . . . the light and glory with which God appears surrounded in the gospel is especially the glory of his love and covenant grace.[13]

---

[12]Edwards, "The Miscellanies," in *Works*, 13:496.
[13]Edwards, "Ethical Writings," in *Works*, 8:145.

Thus the idea that God's glory might be something different in God, at odds with his love, is a complete misunderstanding. For his glory is not about taking but giving. "Love is the light and glory which are about the throne on which God sits." John Owen wrote that God "glorifies himself *in the communication of all good things.*"[14] Indeed— and particularly in the communication, the sharing, of himself.

Christ the True Light, 1527 (by Hans Holbein the Younger)

But wait a moment: in the exodus, God glorifies himself through *judging* Egypt; in Exodus, "the glory of the LORD looked like a consuming fire" (Ex 24:17). That looks like a very different sort of glory. In fact it is not. One of the loveliest things about light is that it overcomes and banishes darkness. Once, Jonathan Edwards was preaching on Christ as the sun of righteousness from this passage, the beginning of Malachi 4:

> "Surely the day is coming; it will burn like a furnace. All the arrogant and every evildoer will be stubble, and that day that is coming will set them on fire," says the LORD Almighty. "Not a root or a branch will be left to them. But for you who revere my name, the sun of righteousness will rise with healing in its wings." (Mal 4:1-2)

The main lesson Edwards drew from it was that "that same spir-

---

[14]John Owen, "Exposition of Hebrews," in *The Works of John Owen*, ed. William H. Goold, 24 vols. (1850-1855; republished, Edinburgh: Banner of Truth, 1965-1991), 23:99, my emphasis.

itual Sun, whose beams are most comfortable and beneficial to believers, will burn and destroy unbelievers."[15] It is the same light, the same glory. But the very glory that is the fragrance of life to some is the smell of death to others. God's purpose is unfathomably kind: he will at the last so spread his life, being and goodness that he will be all in all; he will at the last fill the universe with the light of his wonderful glory. He is all light—but that *is* terrible for those who love the darkness.

The Glory of the LORD Was Standing There

The glory of God is like a shining light; but in Ezekiel 1 the appearance of the glory also looks like a man (see also Ezek 3:23).

Or, as Hebrews 1:3 puts it, "The Son is the radiance of God's glory." That, in fact, is the reason why God's glory is outgoing and radiant: because it is a Trinitarian thing. The Son—the light of the world—is the splendor of the Father, the shining out of the Father's bright glory. As such, Jesus *is* the glory and weight of God: he goes *out* from the Father exactly showing us just what the very being of the Father is like. And as Ezekiel saw, just like his Father he is radiant. In fact, the Son *is* the radiance of his Father.

Woodcut of Ezekiel 1 from the Wittenberg Bible (Lucas Cranach the Younger)

Now when we see that Jesus is the radiance of God's glory, it becomes impossible to think that God's glory is something that is

---

[15]Edwards, "Sermons and Discourses, 1739-1742," in *Works*, 22:52.

not about love. Through Jesus, the Father shows us his innermost being—in the form of a servant, dying to give us life. And it is *as* Jesus comes to us from heaven, making himself nothing, that he displays his glory. "The Word became flesh and made his dwelling among us. We have seen his glory, the glory of the One and Only, who came from the Father, full of grace and truth" (Jn 1:14). Through Jesus we do not see a proud divine glory, but the glory of inexpressible humility and kindness.

Think of how Jesus shows his glory. At the wedding in Cana, he "revealed his glory" (Jn 2:11). How? By turning water into the best wine. Then he is "glorified" by raising Lazarus from the dead (Jn 11:4). Now it is not that Jesus did those things to become a celebrity like some touring magician. It is that through those things he makes himself known as the compassionate one with the ability to heal, to bring life and rich abundance. Then the Spirit "glorifies" him by, as he says, "taking from what is mine and making it known to you" (Jn 16:14). He shares, is fruitful, and so makes his disciples fruitful—and this too "glorifies" his Father (Jn 15:8). He is made known as fruitful.

But all that is just a prelude to "the hour" of his glorification. In John 12, Jesus announces that "the hour has come for the Son of Man to be glorified." What can he mean?

> "I tell you the truth, unless a grain of wheat falls to the ground and dies, it remains only a single seed. But if it dies, it produces many seeds. . . . Now is the time for judgment on this world; now the prince of this world will be driven out. But I, when I am lifted up from the earth, will draw all men to myself." He said this to show the kind of death he was going to die. (Jn 12:23-33)

Jesus is the glory of his Father, shining out from the Father and perfectly enlightening us to see what the Father is really like. And now Jesus himself is to be glorified. That is, we are now going to see his innermost being and weight displayed. What does it look like? A seed, dying to bear fruit. For he was speaking of his death. Astonishingly, the moment when Jesus finally reaches the deepest point of his humiliation, at the cross, is the moment when he is glorified and most clearly seen for who he is. On the cross we see the glorification of the glory of God, the deepest revelation of the very heart of God—and it is all about laying down his own life to give life, to bear fruit. The Reformer John Calvin wrote that "in the cross of Christ, as in a magnificent theatre, the inestimable goodness of God is displayed before the whole world. In all the creatures, indeed, both high and low, the glory of God shines, but nowhere has it shone more brightly than in the cross."[16]

Woodcut of the crucifixion from the Gustav Vasa Bible, 1526

Here is a glory no other God would want. Other gods *need* worship and service and sustenance. But this God needs nothing. He has life in himself—and so much so that he is brimming over. His glory is inestimably good, overflowing, self-giving.

"God Is Dead"

In 1882 Friedrich Nietzsche boldly announced the death of God. By that he meant that belief in God is simply no longer viable. He meant it to be an end to all faith. In actual fact, though, "God is dead" is where true faith begins. For, on the cross, Christ the

---

[16]John Calvin, *Commentary on John* (Edinburgh: Calvin Translation Society, 1844-1856; repr., Grand Rapids: Baker, 1993), 13.31.

Glory puts to death all false ideas of God; and as he cries out to his Father and offers himself up by the Spirit (Heb 9:14), breathing out his last, he reveals a God beyond our dreams.

Through the cross we see a God who is infinitely better. There we do not see a God who does not care about our plight; we see one who personally deals with the root of it all. The Babylonian god Marduk said he wanted humanity to exist as his slaves. Jesus said he "did not come to be served, but to serve, and to give his life as a ransom for many" (Mk 10:45).

And so we come to where we started: Jesus Christ as the bright lane to knowledge of the true God. As the glorious, Spirit-anointed Son, he reveals his Father. He reveals God to be Father, Son and Spirit—and thus he reveals the only God who is love, and he shows us the true glory of that love on the cross. In him we see a God far beyond the bores and tyrants we all rush to reject. In him we see the good God. And how good he is!

Conclusion

NO OTHER CHOICE

What is your Christian life like? What is the shape of your gospel, your faith? In the end, it will all depend on what you think God is like. Who God is drives everything. So what is the human problem? Is it merely that we have strayed from a moral code? Or is it something worse: that we have strayed from *him*? What is salvation? Is it merely that we are brought back as law-abiding citizens? Or is it something better: that we are brought back as *beloved children*? What is the Christian life about? Mere behavior? Or something deeper: *enjoying* God? And then there's what our churches are like, our marriages, our relationships, our mission: all are molded in the deepest way by what we think of God.

In the early fourth century, Arius went for a precooked God, ready-baked in his mind. Ignoring the way, the truth and life, he defined God *without the Son,* and the fallout was catastrophic: without the Son, God cannot truly be a Father; thus alone, he is not truly love. Thus he can have no fellowship to share with us, no Son to bring us close, no Spirit through whom we might know him. Arius was left with a very thin gruel: a life of self-dependent effort under the all-seeing eye of his distant and loveless God.

The tragedy is that we all think like Arius every day. We think of God without the Son. We think of "God," and not the Father of the Son. But from there it really doesn't take long before you find that *you* are just a whole lot more interesting than *this* "God." And could you but see yourself, you would notice that you are fast becoming like this "God": all inward-looking and fruitless. The twentieth-century Russian theologian Vladimir Lossky put it like this: "If we reject the Trinity as the sole ground of all reality and all thought, we are committed to a road that leads nowhere; we end in an aporia [a despair], in folly, in the disintegration of our being, in spiritual death. Between the Trinity and hell there lies no other choice."[1]

However, starting with Jesus, Athanasius found himself with a God who could not have been more different from the God of Arius. It wasn't that he found himself with some extra small print in his description of God ("the Trinity"): Athanasius had a God of love, a kind Father who draws us to share his eternal love and fellowship.

The choice remains: Which God will we have? Which God will we proclaim? Without Jesus the Son, we cannot know that God is truly a loving Father. Without Jesus the Son, we cannot know him as *our* loving Father. But as Luther discovered, through Jesus we may know that God is a Father, and "we may look into His fatherly heart and sense how boundlessly He loves us. That would warm our hearts, setting them aglow."[2] Yes it would, and more: it would bring about reformation.

---

[1]Vladimir Lossky, *The Mystical Theology of the Eastern Church* (Cambridge: James Clarke, 1957), p. 66.
[2]Martin Luther, *Luther's Large Catechism* (St. Louis: Concordia, 1978), p. 70.

Image Credits

Introduction

Conversion of Paravas by Francis Xavier in 1542: Wikimedia Commons <http://commons.wikimedia.org/wiki/File:Conversion_of_Paravas_by_Francis_Xavier_in_1542.jpg >.

Chapter 1

Icon of St. Athanasius: Wikimedia Commons <http://commons.wiki media.org/wiki/File:Athanasius_I.jpg>.

The Baptism of Christ by Master E. S.: Wikimedia Commons <http://commons.wikimedia.org/wiki/File:Die_Taufe_Christi.png>.

Richard of St. Victor in an illustration from Dante's **Paradiso:** Wikimedia Commons <http://commons.wikimedia.org/wiki/File:Dante_Pd10_BL_Yates_Thompson_36_f147.jpg>.

Ordination of St. Hilarius (Hilary of Poitiers): Wikimedia Commons <http://commons.wikimedia.org/wiki/File:Hilaryofpoitiers.jpg>.

Chapter 2

Marduk: Wikimedia Commons <http://commons.wikimedia.org/wiki/File:Marduk_and_pet.jpg>.

Aristotle: Wikimedia Commons <http://commons.wikimedia.org/wiki/File:Aristotle.jpg>.

Hell by the Master of Catherine of Cleves: Wikimedia Commons <http://commons.wikimedia.org/wiki/File:Hellmouth.jpg>.

Richard Sibbes: Wikimedia Commons <http://commons.wikimedia.org/wiki/File:RichardSibbes.jpg>.

Creation of Eve: Scan courtesy of the author.

Johann Sebastian Bach: Wikimedia Commons <http://commons.wikimedia.org/wiki/File:Johann_Sebastian_Bach.jpg>.

Chapter 3

Adam and Eve in The Seven Deadly Sins, *an illustration in Giovanni Boccaccio's* De claris mulieribus (On Famous Women): Wikimedia Commons   <http://commons.wikimedia.org/wiki/File:De_claris_mulieribus_001.jpg>.

Conversion of Augustine by Benozzo Gozzoli: Wikimedia Commons <http://commons.wikimedia.org/wiki/File:TolleLege.jpg>.

Illustration of the high priest offering a sacrifice of a goat on the Day of Atonement, from Treasures of the Bible *by Henry Davenport Northrop:* Wikimedia Commons <http://commons.wikimedia.org/wiki/File:High_Priest_Offering_Sacrifice_of_a_Goat.jpg>.

Illustration of the consecration of Aaron and his sons from the Holman Bible of 1890: Wikimedia Commons <http://commons.wikimedia.org/wiki/File:Holman_Consecration_of_Aaron_and_His_Sons.jpg>.

Martin Luther as a monk: Wikimedia Commons <http://commons.wikimedia.org/wiki/File:Luther_with_tonsure.gif>.

Illustration of St. Matthew from the 9th century, writing his Gospel: Wikimedia Commons <http://commons.wikimedia.org/wiki/File:Saint_Matthew2.jpg>.

Chapter 4

William Tyndale portrait from Foxe's Book of Martyrs: Wikimedia Commons <http://commons.wikimedia.org/wiki/File:William_Tyndale.jpg>.

John Calvin: Wikimedia Commons <http://commons.wikimedia.org/wiki/File:John_Calvin_03.jpg>.

Cardinal Sadoleto: Wikimedia Commons <http://commons.wikimedia.org/wiki/File:Cardinal_Sadoleto.jpg>.

Moses showing the Ten Commandments, by Gustave Doré: Wikimedia

Commons <http://commons.wikimedia.org/wiki/File:Moses_radiant .jpg>.

Woodcut of the return of the prodigal son: Wikimedia Commons <http:// commons.wikimedia.org/wiki/File:Schnorr_von_Carolsfeld_Bibel_ in_Bildern_1860_198.png>.

John Owen: Wikimedia Commons <http://commons.wikimedia.org/ wiki/File:JohnOwenFrontispiece.jpg>.

Thomas Chalmers: Wikimedia Commons <http://commons.wikimedia .org/wiki/File:Thomas_Chalmers_-_Project_Gutenberg_13103.jpg>.

Chapter 5

Friedrich Schleiermacher: Wikimedia Commons <http://commons.wiki media.org/wiki/File:Friedrich_Daniel_Ernst_Schleiermacher.jpg>.

Thor: Wikimedia Commons <http://commons.wikimedia.org/wiki/ File:Christmas_throughout_Christendom_-_Thor.png>.

Creation of light by Gustave Doré: Wikimedia Commons <http:// commons.wikimedia.org/wiki/File:Creation_of_Light.png>.

Christ as the true light by Hans Holbein the Younger, 1526: Wikimedia Commons <http://www.wikipaintings.org/en/hans-holbein-the-younger /christ-as-the-true-light p. 125>.

Woodcut of Ezekiel 1 by Lucas Cranach the Younger: Scan courtesy of the author.

Crucifixion scene from the New Testament in Swedish, 1526: Wikimedia Commons <http://commons.wikimedia.org/wiki/File:NT_1526_004 .png>.

Note: All images from Wikimedia Commons are in the public domain.

Scripture Index

Finding the Textbook You Need